HUMAN AND GLOBAL SECURITY: AN EXPLORATION OF TERMS

Peter J. Stoett

There is growing recognition that the post–Cold War era demands new conceptions of human and global security. In this highly readable account of international security issues, Peter Stoett begins by discussing four principal security threats: state violence, environmental degradation, population displacement, and globalization.

Employing a minimalist–maximalist framework – the minimalist interpretation applies to conventional and restricted legal definitions of a term, while the maximalist interpretation refers to broader conceptions of problems, often global in effect – Stoett argues that the acceptance of either perspective has profound conceptual and immediate praxiological implications. While the latter regards security in terms of the state and governance within an international system, it is the former, more specific, interpretation that is suitable for policy analysis. A fundamental and varied understanding of the basic terms of global security, Stoett reasons, is crucial to meaningful critical debate on matters of contemporary world politics.

The concluding chapter on globalization, with its examination of environment issues and population displacement, situates human and global security within the larger context of the historical process of expansionism. *Human and Global Security* provides a sophisticated, yet accessible study of contemporary security issues within the context of international relations theory. Its approach will appeal to a general audience as well as students and scholars.

PETER J. STOETT is Assistant Professor, Department of Political Science, Concordia University.

Human and Global Security:
An Exploration of Terms

Peter Stoett

UNIVERSITY OF TORONTO PRESS
Toronto Buffalo London

© University of Toronto Press Incorporated 1999
Toronto Buffalo London
Printed in Canada

ISBN 0-8020-4746-7 (cloth)
ISBN 0-8020-8304-8 (paper)

Printed on acid-free paper

Canadian Cataloguing in Publication Data

Stoett, Peter John, 1965–
Human and global security : an exploration of terms

Includes bibliographical references and index.
ISBN 0-8020-4746-7 (bound)   ISBN 0-8020-8304-8 (pbk.)

1. International relations – Terminology.   2. World politics –
Terminology.   3. International relations – Philosophy.
4. World politics – Philosophy.   I. Title.

JZ1161.S76 1999   327.1'01'4   C99-931386-X

This book has been published with the help of a grant from the Humanities
and Social Sciences Federation of Canada, using funds provided by the
Social Sciences and Humanities Research Council of Canada.

The University of Toronto Press acknowledges the financial assistance to its
publishing program of the Canada Council for the Arts and the Ontario Arts
Council.

University of Toronto Press acknowledges the financial support for its
publishing activities of the Government of Canada through the Book
Publishing Industry Development Program (BPIDP).

Canadä

Contents

Preface

This book takes to task the popular notion that post–Cold War international politics calls for a new security agenda. It does not challenge that idea, but rather seeks to strengthen it with a discussion of four principal threats to human and global security today: state violence, environmental degradation, population displacement, and globalization. This is not to imply that inter-state warfare is impossible, or even unlikely, in the future, or that we should be at all complacent about conventional terrorism, border disputes, weapons of mass destruction, and other sources of instability. Rather, in the book I attempt to explore, through a minimalist–maximalist framework that focuses on narrow and broad definitions of several key terms, the nature of the contemporary security dilemma.

One hears much about *human security* these days. Post–Cold War governments use this concept as a conceptual hanger on which new and old defence agendas can be aired. In the past decade an academic discourse has materialized centred on the question of what security can and does mean today. But we still need to follow through with the promise that discourse offers. We need, in other words, more specificity, lest potentially progressive terms such as human security end up suffering from the affliction of conceptual promiscuity and thereby become devalued. In the same way, *global security*, a term that promises some escape from the state-centricity of more limited security preoccupations, remains an embryonic term in need of conceptual nourishment.

This book derives from several attempts to achieve greater conceptual clarity for terms that students and teachers alike in the field of world politics will no doubt struggle with in the post–Cold War era. We can also explore human and global security as concepts, and as conceptual umbrellas for what we come to define as threats. There is no escaping a very basic fact: the human mind operates with symbols, some of which we have called words, and these words in turn shape ideas about what is and what should be. This book will discuss two general perspectives on the terms chosen for analysis: the minimalist and the maximalist. The former applies to conventional and – in cases where relevant international law exists – restricted definitions of terms. The latter refers to broader conceptions of problems – problems that are often global in effect – and thus to the need for more ambitious initiatives or responses, usually through international organizations such as the United Nations. Minimalists seek specificity, whether in legal or policy terms; while maximalists tend to use terms to connote bigger problems with the state, with governance, and with the international system. Whether we accept a minimalist or a maximalist perspective has both profound conceptual and immediate praxiological implications.

Our terms are chosen because they reflect contemporary crises not only of international relations but also of the human spirit. A new security paradigm will move us away from the guns, bullets, and boats approach (though it is obvious that military prowess continues to be a vital characteristic of major powers), and focus our attention on individuals and threatened communities. Arguably, these are threatened the most by gross human rights violations such as genocide and mass displacement, and by environmental destruction, which threatens the very essence of our survival, our habitat. With this in mind, the book examines three key terms – genocide, ecocide, and refugee – that seem to capture all these threats, including the threat of becoming stateless. And we add one more term, which (arguably again) ties the first three all together within the context of a discussion of contemporary global security: globalization. Having attained varied understandings of these concepts, we will be able to see operationalized some of the broader points made by the security debate, and such a discussion will advance the reader's awareness of general issues in world politics, while permitting specialists to continue a critical debate.

We begin by looking at *genocide*, which – as Rwanda, the Sudan, and Bosnia forcefully suggest – is still very much with us as we move into the twenty-first century. There can be no greater direct threat to groups of people, and the fact that states are generally complicit in the act makes it a discussion with many uncertain implications for state sovereignty and justice. After this we explore the related concept of *ecocide*, which was so prominent during the Gulf War military display but may also apply to a much broader ecological crisis indicated by such threats as global warming and ozone depletion. (One might argue that the antidote to ecocide is *sustainable development*, an equally nebulous term that we will return to in this book.) From this, we will consider the term *refugee*, a key concept that will always be present in any political system whose chief units are divided along territorial lines. Strict definitions of refugee may be outmoded in today's geopolitical climate; that being said, the term may be the only one capable of generating a sustained humanitarian response. The real point is that large population movements are a certainty, and this is a central concern to the state system and to individuals who find themselves stateless. Finally, we discuss what has emerged as the 1990s buzzword, *globalization*, which is often taken as synonymous with a neoliberal, corporate agenda (the ideology of internationalized capital), but can also be taken to mean imperialism or, even, technological convergence. I will argue that ultimately, we must consider our understanding of globalization as the contemporary manifestation of a historical process of expansionism, and that we must also consider its negative accompaniments: state violence, environmental degradation, and population displacement.

Chapter 1 discusses the importance of terminology in world politics, and then introduces the security debate. This chapter is not intended to be definitive in this regard, since the debate has been carried on elsewhere for quite some time now. A *human security* framework suggests that our concern with the survival of individuals and groups, and not just states, requires us to take a closer look at terms that are used with increasing frequency, but that are too often treated as working assumptions rather than as contestable concepts in and of themselves. Nowhere is this more evident than with the term 'globalization' – which has come to mean so much that one wonders if it means anything anymore – but we'll see that all the terms explored here have been subject to a very expansive, *maximalist* definition which, one might argue, renders them meaningless. On the other hand, those who insist on a narrow, legal, or *minimalist* definition may lose sight of the broader picture, of the extent of related problems we face today. Each succeeding chapter in this book will describe the minimalist and maximalist conceptions of a term, and discuss their institutional and ethical implications. It is my hope that such a discussion will take the reader on a journey across much of the empirical and theoretical landscape of contemporary world politics.

This book derives from earlier thinking and related publications as I make my own way across that troubled landscape. Having published articles dealing with all of these issues, I became consumed by an urge to tie them together in some cogent fashion, under one roof as it were, in order not only to clarify my own thinking but also to encourage serious debate among interested scholars, students, and other readers. I freely admit that the following are exploratory essays, but I also wish to stress here that the terms evaluated have institutional implications. Generally, I find myself (rather to my surprise) favouring the minimalist perspectives, if largely for pragmatic reasons. But at no point should this be conceived as a project designed to delegitimize the maximalist perspectives, which provide us with intriguing and inspirational modes of thought, if not concrete solutions. Taken as a whole they serve to sophisticate and challenge conventional, state-centric understandings of security; and they caution those who have a reflexive enthusiasm for globalization.

This book was written over the space of several years, and in that time I have incurred substantial intellectual debts to colleagues, students, and friends alike. I want to thank for their persistence two editors at University of Toronto Press: Virgil Duff and Siobhan McMenemy. Several anonymous reviewers provided by UTP and the Aid to Scholarly Publishing Programme provided substantive critiques of earlier drafts; and several others did the same with individual chapters, in particular Kim Nossal, Evan Potter, Simon Dalby, and Kim Cowan. Naturally, any errors are my responsibility. Shane Mulligan offered a comprehensive critique, and Matthew Kudelka an equally careful copy edit.

I completed the manuscript while I was settling into the Department of Political Science at Concordia University in Montreal, and I am particularly grateful to the new Chair there, Reeta Tremblay, for her support and understanding. As usual, my daughter Alexandra provided inspiration, and my parents, sisters, and close friends were invaluable.

I dedicate this book to a departed friend, colleague, and (most of all) teacher, Professor Bill Graf. His inquisitive mind and strong sense of social justice have been a formative feature of my own development, and his premature passing was a painful reminder of the fragility of human life.

HUMAN AND GLOBAL SECURITY:
AN EXPLORATION OF TERMS

1

Terminology and Security in World Politics

term: 1. *n.* word used to express definite concept, esp. in branch of study etc;

The Oxford Dictionary of Current English (1986), 776

The above quote is deceptive, for there are few *definite* concepts in life, and even fewer in the study of political science. This book proceeds under the weight of that fact and is based on two essential premises.

First, words matter, yet most words have many meanings. Defining words is a fundamental act, for us as individuals and as members of collectives. When definitions are constructed in a closed and limited fashion, alternative thinking can be stifled and orthodoxy can be reinforced. By the same token, the act of exploring the definitions of words is a robust pedagogical process, capable of fostering the creative spirit and pushing academic discourse farther along its path of self-discovery.

Second, as we enter a new and uncertain century, we need to continue rethinking the meaning of one term in particular: *security.* Most reconceptualizations of this term have involved reintroducing quite old and noble ideas about protecting individuals and collectivities from harm. The Westphalian system forced modern thinkers to posit the state as the centre of that protection; but recent decades have challenged this ontological primacy and its corresponding praxiology as well. One might argue that predominant Western thought has led to this: the liberal tradition, despite its Hegelian and nationalist inclinations, views the state as the means to security and not as the end. But within the field of international relations the shift in emphasis away from state-centric thinking has occurred side by side with empirical developments: the rise of crises that defy unilateral and even multilateral management.

Several factors make this an optimum time to deal with the subject of security, but we can link them all with its a simple statement: these are insecure times. We live, as James Rosenau has suggested, with turbulence; and in an era when uncountable actors are transforming the political landscape with remarkable speed, and when societies are struggling to find their developmental direction. If, as many sages have long argued, we fear the unknown most, then we should be very afraid indeed. Who knows where post–Cold War power configurations are leading us? And what level of resource strain the earth can accommodate? And what long-term effects globalization will have? And whether the state survive, or die a peaceful death, or wreak violence on citizens? The overriding impression is of a great experimental machine with no one at the controls. What's a political scientist to do?

Before we can claim a genuine perspective on the term *global security*, perhaps we need to explore the continued causes of insecurity. What threats are prevalent today, and what threats will arise in the near future? We face an unlimited number of them, from narcoterrorism to pension fund misinvestments. If we are to move beyond a realist interpretation of world politics, in which states fear other states and seek military comfort, we must take seriously threats to security that are often minimized in the field of world politics. This book will deal with four related threats to human and global security: state violence, environmental degradation, population displacement, and globalization. It will be argued that these terms, each representative of empirical crises or rapid periods of change, also represent a broader crisis of the human spirit; that together they can capture the essence of the troubled times ahead; and that they all have immediate and long-term implications for international institutions and relations as well as profound impact on individuals and groups.

In keeping with the pedagogical spirit outlined earlier, we narrow the terms to four: *genocide, ecocide, refugee,* and *globalization*; and explore each in their narrowest and broadest interpretations.

Terms in World Politics

The study of world politics today revolves, as it always has, around a stable of core concepts. Some of these are ephemeral, reflecting fads of the day; others are seemingly perennial. For example, *anarchy* has long been a central term used by political theorists trying to explain war. This word normally connotes a society crumbling in disarray. A modern example was the state of Somalia, where in 1992 there was in effect no central government but rather various factions fighting – often in the streets of Mogadishu – for the right to control various regions of the country. In this vein, *Oxford* defines anarchy as 'disorder, especially political; lack of government.'[1] Students of world politics are constantly looking at a world that is without a central source of authority; and as a result, anarchy becomes for many of them the central defining characteristic of the international system.[2] This lack of authority at the international level, in a system comprised of self-protective and often hostile units named states, means at the least that some form of war between states is always possible, if not likely.

Yet one can argue, with Hedley Bull, that in the international context anarchy is not synonymous with disorder because over time states 'form a society in the sense that they conceive themselves to be bound by a common set of rules in their relations with one another, and share in the working of common institutions.'[3] Even a balance of power, based on preparations for war, may be viewed as such a commonality; and so might world domination by a key state in a condition often referred to as *hegemonic stability*.[4] Others, meanwhile, suggest that this essential anarchy is compromised by the establishment of patterns of co-operation between states, or what have come to be termed *regimes*. The definition of this term seems to fluctuate according to research agendas, but the main point is that the potentially disastrous effects of global anarchy can be mitigated by the evolution of institutions or regimes that have some level of autonomous influence, so that an effective, central authority in world politics need not develop concurrently.[5] Still others would take anarchy as a very positive term, suggesting that people must live free from the imposition of state hierarchy.

Of course, *most* of the major terms employed in the field are still contestable. After contrasting the late-nineteenth-century work of Bishop Stubbs and Richard Cobden on the term *balance of power*, Ernst Haas wrote: 'One writer is certain that the concept holds the key to understanding modern history; the other is equally convinced that it never had any actual historical existence at all.'[6] During the Cold War it was fairly well accepted that a rough balance of power existed between the two superpowers, reinforced by strategies of nuclear deterrence. Presently, however, no one is too sure whether we live in a unipolar or a multipolar world (this depends on one's estimation of American power – and, for that matter, on one's operational definition of power itself).

Similarly, political scientists from various subdisciplines have argued over the meaning of *sovereignty*. Does it imply territorial integrity, and autonomy from outside influence? Is it primarily a legal concept denoting the ultimate source of political authority in a given jurisdiction? Does it lay with the people, or citizenry? Or is it a term employed by ruling classes to hegemonize, or legitimize, unjust power relations? Sovereignty is associated with nationalism, but is it therefore diminished in some quantitative or qualitative sense as the state plays a less obvious role in the global economy? Millions of people have died defending sovereignty, yet we lack a clear consensus as to what the word means. We will return to it, however, in each of the chapters that follow, as well as in our discussion of security below.[7]

Another term that is subject to various interpretations, and yet is widely used in the present-day literature, is *multilateralism*. There are several dominant images of multilateralism within the policymaking, public, and academic communities. How a trade analyst employs the term will differ from how a military strategic analyst does. Others are more concerned with the comparatively mundane aspects of co-ordinating policy so that states are better able to implement policies with international linkages; still others view multilateralism as an extension of old-style Western imperialism. The definition of multilateralism generally accepted in the present day is that it concerns arrangements between three or more states and involves diffuse reciprocity, nondiscrimination, and indivisibility; in contrast, bilateralism (diplomacy between two states) 'is premised on specific reciprocity, the simultaneous balancing of specific quids pro quos by each party with every other at all times.'[8] But one might also view multilateralism as joint efforts at preventive diplomacy, or peacekeeping, or, in matters of collective security, the collective punishment of aggressive states.

The study of multilateralism might also be considered synonymous with *global policy studies*, or 'the study of international interactions designed to deal with shared public policy problems,' such as transboundary issues, common property dilemmas, and 'simultaneous problems' such as health, education, and welfare, 'about which all countries can learn from each other.'[9] In a remarkably less benign image, multilateralism can be seen as hegemonic managerialism, the mechanism by which leading capitalist states maintain an unjust world order based on the North's exploitation of the South. Similarly, there are markedly varied definitions of the term *trilateralism*, which may be used to denote the co-ordinated, or conflictive, efforts of three states involved in an economic/diplomatic process, such as Canada, the United States, and Mexico in the North American Free Trade Agreement. But others use the term irrespective of the three-state limit that 'trilateral' would seem to impose. The Trilateral Commission is a forum created to discuss co-operation questions between North America, Western Europe, and Japan. Here the reference is in essence to three economic power centres.

Moving beyond both state and regional formulae, Stephen Gill defines trilateralism as 'the project of developing an organic (or relatively permanent) alliance between the major capitalist states, with the aim of promoting (or sustaining) a stable form of world order which is congenial to their dominant interests.'[10]

Anarchy, balance of power, regime, sovereignty, multilateralism: these are certainly some of the more central concepts in the study of world politics today. This book will advance the argument, however, that there are a host of other terms – four of which will capture our immediate attention – that are as important, not only because they present us with similarly contestable conceptual horizons, but also because they reflect contemporary concerns about human and global security. All of these terms, meanwhile, must be placed in the context of an international system – or to use a more positive if again highly contestable term, an *international society* or *community* – in which the problems of anarchy and the prospects of institutions and regimes figure prominently. The principle of sovereignty, which implies the right of nation-states to territorial integrity, remains dominant in the official United Nations universe. However, significant international organizations, including the UN itself, have developed in the last century; and these institutions, though far from establishing global governments, do have an impact on world affairs and on the domestic affairs of states. Furthermore, many commentators argue that we should continue to expand their influence, despite the challenges to the UN's legitimacy posed by the failure of peacekeeping missions in the Balkans and Africa.[11]

More broadly, there has been an ongoing debate among those who study world politics about what, precisely, they are studying in the first place. There are many points of view that challenge the dominant discourse, which revolves around investigating interstate conflicts. Popular terms in conventional study have included *balance of power, idealism, realism, interdependency*, and others that refer students to the prevailing (though often questioned) wisdom of the day. The challenges to this lexicon are reflected in the rapidly expanding literature that focuses on questions other than order in the world system – though we might argue that they all deal with order itself at some stage. In the context of this book, we see the increased use of terms that previously had little currency in mainstream academia – terms such as *gender, information technology, narrative, ecoholism, ecofeminism, modernity, post-hegemony,* and a virtual semantic buffet of others, all with multiple meanings that vary according to who is using them and when and why they are used. With due respect for the innovative forays these terms offer into traditional international relations theory, in many respects they are not new. Rather, they emphasize the newfound importance, both in the discipline and in policymaking circles, of concerns with justice, ethnicity, gender equality, the environment, and other aspects of life – concerns that have always been with us but have been overshadowed by what the discipline long considered the bigger questions of war and military security.[12] Above and beyond the rather esoteric debates[13] about ontological referents and epistemological implications, these terms have surfaced – or in many cases *re*surfaced – because of terrifyingly rapid changes in the international system itself. That is, there is a dialectic relationship between what we see and what we say; the two feed off each other, leaving a great deal of analytic confusion in their wake but hovering at all times around a redefined conceptualization of yet another great perennial and greatly debated term: security.

This book seeks to train our focus on what are in fact very old concepts: human rights, environmental security, statelessness, and the spread of Western civilization. In order to operationalize this agenda, we will examine four terms in detail. The first is *genocide,* which – as recent events in Rwanda, the Sudan, and Bosnia forcefully suggest – is still very much with us as we move into the twenty-first century. The recent detention of Chile's ex-leader General Pinochet by the United Kingdom (for possible extradition to Spain, where he has been indicted for crimes against humanity and genocide), and the establishment of a war crimes tribunal at the Hague, have refocused our attention on genocide as a crime perpetrated by individuals *through* the state.

Next we explore the concept of *ecocide*, which was so prominent during the 1990–91 Gulf War, with its televized images of burning oil fields, but which may also apply to a much broader ecological crisis in which threats such as global warming and ozone layer depletion figure prominently. Again this is not a new term; it surfaced initially during the United States' military campaign in Vietnam.

After that, we will examine a key concept that will always be present in any system in which the chief units are based on territory: *refugee*. Massive population movements tend to be perceived, rightly or wrongly, as major threats to national security; but one can certainly argue, from the perspective of refugees themselves, that being stateless is a threat to individual security as well. Thus in Chapter 4 we will explore the concept of displacement, as well as the contemporarily popular term 'environmental refugee.' Finally, in our concluding chapter, we will discuss the most conspicuous buzzword of the last decades of this century, *globalization*. Some would argue that the greatest threat facing humanity is the spread of Western values and technology, wherein the local is destroyed in the interests of the global and we all become dangerously dependent on market forces beyond conscious human control. But there are other ways of viewing globalization – for example, as a relatively benign process of trade liberalization – that we will explore as well. With this chapter we move beyond questions of individual, group, or even environmental security, to consider global security; but as we'll see, the differences between these may be an apparition. All of these terms have been selected for their illustrative complexity and current applicability, and for their relationship to a contemporary understanding of human and environmental security.

Several factors tie these terms together. All of them inform the broader debate over what global security means in the post–Cold War era. Each presents fascinating angles on the maximalist definition of security – for example, they raise profound present-day questions related to human rights, environmental security, and the evolution of global society. And there are gaping discrepancies in how they are used in common parlance. The term globalization seems to be in use everywhere (which in itself can lead to the false conclusion that the process of globalization is also everywhere). The term ecocide is still somewhat unusual, though that, unfortunately, may change. It is not uncommon to see the word genocide used to describe small outbreaks of violence, usually in civil warfare; and people fleeing such conflicts are habitually labelled refugees by the press, whether or not they have crossed borders.

Taken together, this inevitably arbitrary choice of terms implies an agenda that is focused on a broader definition of security than that which dominated the discourse in international relations during the Cold War. Each of the first three terms deals with rather extreme cases where, it can be asserted, the nation-state system has failed to deal with the relevant issues, or at least has not wholly succeeded in doing so. Our last term is perhaps the most contested, since globalization is coming to mean so many things to so many people. It is argued here that an understanding of globalization as a progressive concept – if such a thing remains possible after its ideological kidnapping by corporate interests – must take human rights, environmental rights, and refugee rights (obviously these are not mutually exclusive categories!) into consideration. In other words, achieving global security today must involve considering the environmental and human rights issues raised by the blight upon humanity represented by genocide, the threat to human and environmental health presented by ecocide, and the instability and inhumanity generated by the refugee crisis. Unfortunately, it is predictable that in some final form, each of these terms will remain within the lexicon of world politics as another new-yet-old age dawns. For that reason, it is instructive to look at them now, from the vantage point of the closing of one of the most transformative centuries in the history of human civilization.

A Rough Framework

This volume is not intended as an addition to the vast literature on the history of terms in social science, though we will be engaged in a limited amount of etymology. Nor, in case the reader was becoming increasingly concerned (or anxious) with this possibility, is it a contribution to the postmodernist genre that, as explicitly as such a thing is possible, deconstructs the social consequences of dominant discourses and other things. Our main efforts will be to identify some key terms symbolizing events, people, and states of affairs that affect human rights and environmental security in the contemporary international system; to explore some key perspectives of those terms; and then to discuss their conceptual and institutional implications. All of the terms will also be related to the broader issue of global security – a term we will examine in more depth in this introductory chapter.

Most terms used in the social sciences have more than one meaning. We can place these different meanings along a spectrum, with highly restricted meanings, which usually conform to legal and/or more conventional definitions or understandings, at one end; and very broad, or expanded, and often unconventional meanings at the other. These are referred to as *minimalist* and *maximalist* conceptions, respectively. Minimalist understandings will be limited to what is currently the prevalent definition in official discourse; these are often lifted from international legal instruments such as treaties or from academic works. In public discourse and in the classroom, and in the halls of the UN and elsewhere, the benefit of adhering to rigidly minimalist understandings is that doing so provides relative clarity and allows for more practical possibilities to actually do something about problems that inherently involve the state. Maximalist understandings, on the other hand, tend to suggest that there is widespread state complicity in human and environmental rights problems, and are seen as extreme positions by diplomats and more traditional scholars. However, maximalist understandings serve as intriguing heuristic devices, since they challenge conventional wisdom and our analytic imaginations. This is of great pedagogical value.

Each of the terms in this study can be viewed from either end of the continuum. Genocide can refer to a very specific crime perpetrated by states against certain groups, or it can be used to describe that state of inhumanity which allows a world in which millions of children die of simple, malnutrition-related diseases. Ecocide can be viewed as a methodology of warfare, as the Vietnam case suggests; or as a broader process of anthropogenic-induced environmental degradation that is limiting the ability of future generations to enjoy the planet. Refugees have long been defined according to a legal definition that focuses on political persecution; however, one could define them in the broader sense as people forced to move by economic and environmental circumstances. Finally, globalization can be defined as a GATT-inspired incremental process of trade liberalization, or as a historic, epochal process involving nothing less than a global convergence of values, institutions, and technology.

We are quite sympathetic to the maximalist definitions of these terms, yet they do entail a loss of the specificity so cherished by social scientists. It is not the purpose of this book to conclude in favour of one conception or another, but it can be suggested that the minimalist conceptions make the most sense at this point based on their analytic utility and, importantly, on the practical limitations of the maximalist conceptions. This leads us to another important aspect of the rough framework that threads this book together: the institutional implications of various conceptions of the terms. In the case of genocide and refugees in particular, but also in the case of ecocide and globalization, we ask what the policy implications of terminology are. If the crime of genocide (in its minimalist sense) can be prosecuted, what can the international community do at this point in time about the maximalist understanding? Can we expect multilateral regimes to adapt to environmental problems in order to prevent ecocide? Does it make sense to expand our definition of *refugee* when the UN High Commissioner of Refugees has little ability to deal with an expanded mandate? And are we anywhere close to developing institutions for dealing with the technological, economic, and social consequences of globalization? These are institutional questions that government leaders and transnational actors alike will have to deal with in the upcoming era as they define contemporary security by their actions and (as importantly, though often overlooked in conventional analyses) by their inactions. We turn now to an initial discussion of the concept of security itself.

Toward Human and Environmental Security[14]

security: *n.* secure condition of feeling; thing that guards or guarantees; safety of State, company, etc, against espionage, theft, or other danger; organization for ensuring this; ... [F or L (prec.)]

The Oxford Dictionary of Current English (1976), 675

With notable exceptions, the Cold War maintained a semantic grip on the discipline of international relations, centralizing the vocabulary employed by realists. As it became apparent that the East–West divide was narrowing, it grew increasingly popular to look beyond bipolar security concerns; and after a while, doing so became as 'mainstream' as the old nuclear deterrence debate. The passing of the bipolar international power structure has freed us from that structure's conceptual straightjacket. However protracted the conflicts in the Balkans and Africa, and however great the uncertainties about global markets, a new age seems to be upon us – one rather like the pre–Cold War era – in which multilateral solutions are desperately needed to solve regional problems but are simply not forthcoming. This has coincided with a rise in concern about environmental problems, many of which (ozone depletion, global warming, and so on) have clearly reached global proportions. The importance of non-state actors, both profit oriented and issue oriented, is also increasingly obvious, and here we have yet another radical departure from traditional notions of security. For example, multinational corporations (MNCs) fear threats of expropriation and 'unfair' taxation policies, if present corporate enthusiasm for the OECD-negotiated Multilateral Agreement on Investment (MAI) is any indication. Nongovernmental organizations (NGOs), meanwhile, typically define security as protection from arbitrary state arrest and/or torture, freedom from coerced gender roles, and the avoidance of losing limbs to land mines.

Nonetheless, a minimalist perspective, equating security with the sanctity of national borders, has dominated the field of international relations for a very long time.[15] In part, this reflects the dominance of realism in the American academy, though it is probably fair to say that the perspective broadly labelled *neoliberalism* holds as much sway today.[16] As Seymor Brown insists, human society 'cannot return to the simpler political configurations for assuring public order that prevailed before the twentieth-century revolutions in transportation and communication technology.'[17] Nevertheless, the neoliberal literature, though it focuses attention on nonstate actors and transnational coalitions, makes no pretence about moving beyond what is essentially a state-centric point of view. Scholars promoting a more critical perspective – most of whom would be uncomfortable with the label *neomarxist*, yet who clearly derive many of their basic assumptions from international political economy schools with Marxist roots – have long challenged the state's analytic primacy. They assert the causal significance of classes, capital, and popular movements; while others reject positivism altogether and emphasize the need to understand the various normative factors that conspire to make the world seem as it does.[18]

Throughout this book we will see that when it comes to some key words, adopting a maximalist meaning presents both conceptual and institutional problems. However, and as our forthcoming discussions will indicate, the spectres of genocide, ecocide, mass population movements, and rapid globalization demand that we at least entertain a broader vision, more toward maximalist conceptions of global security. This hardly negates the value or likelihood of determined efforts to preserve territorial integrity. The minimalist conception of security has, in effect, provided the rationale for various instruments of military ideology. Whether or not we accept the implied normative assumption that to do so is in some way sanctimonious, countless millions have died, and have killed, 'for the state.' Firmly embedded institutions – educational, recreational, employment-related, and legal – are dedicated to and dependent upon its preservation, and they are often among the most pervasive influences in people's lives. Direct propaganda assaults are still common in this regard; that being said, in most modern states the subtle yet aggressive approach works best. Even when nationalism isn't overtly manifested in chants and flag waving (and the supposedly spontaneous burning of others' flags), it is assumed to be a latent force – a source of soft power held in strategic reserve for desperate times.

We should say at the outset that one might view a minimalist conception of human security as centred on the individual, in the somewhat ethnocentric tradition of Western ideas about liberty. However, as a bow to the context of our discussion – important and contestable terms in world politics – we are assuming here that the nation-state represents the centre of attention in the minimalist conception of security. The maximalist position, it is argued, urges us to adopt *global security* as the most important goal, and to recognize the importance of questions related to values and justice for nonstate entities – questions that will resurface throughout the next four chapters.[19] A growing body of literature, which we can trace back to the writings of Immanuel Kant and beyond, suggests that it remains a worthy goal. Not only are transnational relations analytically important, but they also help form the building blocks (as opposed to blocs of states!) of global society or international community. And there is a natural convergence between individual human rights and this broad conception of world order.

Of course, those who feel that the term *security* is losing its specificity in academic circles are probably correct; but they hardly need fear the immediate demise of the nation-state as a consequence. Given current divisions and conflicts, any contemplated obsequies – or celebrations – should be indefinitely postponed. There are real conflicts between what human and environmental security *should* mean and what they *can* mean in the policy context of nation-state interactions. As R.J. Vincent wrote, late in his distinguished career, 'we keep the cautious awareness that political power is concentrated at the level of the state, and that any scheme for moral improvement has to find its way in this world of states.'[20] So it also is with the term *security*. Yet the singular importance of broadening an idea that is central to the daily life of every human being, remains.

Minimalist to Maximalist Conceptions of Security

R.B.J. Walker writes that 'the Treaty of Westphalia of 1648 serves as a crucial demarcation between an era still dominated by competing claims to religious universalism and hierarchical authority and an era of secular competition and co-operation among autonomous political communities.'[21] The Peace of Westphalia, which came at the end of the exhausting Thirty Years' War, articulated the principle of sovereign jurisdiction within territorial limits. In the formal and Eurocentric sense, at least, all states were decreed equal, and none would have the right, divine or otherwise, to interfere in the internal affairs of another.[22]

Many years later another document, written after yet another war, the Charter of the United Nations, further entrenched the principle of nonintervention. This was reflective of a canonistic tenet of policymaking, the *national interest*, which was defined primarily in relation to the territorial security of the state. The state as actor mirrors the precarious position of people in the state of nature, which, to quote Thomas Hobbes, is a 'condition of Warre of every man against every man.'[23] This promotes a zero-sum world in which security is obtained at the expense of others. As Robert Ardrey wrote in his controversial *The Territorial Imperative*, the 'predator fights for a net gain in security, whether in loot, land, slaves, or the confusion of enemies. The defender ... fights to conserve security, and to destroy the forces that threaten it.'[24] (The line between predator and defender is a thin one.) Early hypotheses about the territorial state's inevitable obsolescence in the age of the intercontinental nuclear-tipped missile proved premature.[25] Despite impressive forays into arms control, and despite confidence-building measures, preparation for war remained the conventional route for achieving security at this level. This is further evidenced, as opposed to refuted, by the gradual acceptance of the concept of *collective security* at an operational level. Collective security refers to a condition in which states agree essentially to collectively punish aggressors that commit acts of aggression against other states. This system is representative of genuine efforts to avoid a repetition of the two world wars of the 1900s, but it is also quite obviously intended to protect individual states' territorial integrity. (It is also quite selective in terms of what, exactly, is deemed aggressive behaviour.)

The past two decades have seen a multitude of publications that challenge the traditional concept of security as limited to the protection of the political invention termed the nation-state. Very generally, and primarily within Western literary circles (especially as articulated by the Palme Commission), there has been a sustained call for the establishment of *comprehensive* as opposed to *collective* security; and environmental security has become a fixture in the arguments advanced for this shift.[26] There is considerable controversy over this matter, since the concept of national security has a sacred ring to many military analysts and patriots alike, and a negative connotation to many environmentalists and human rights activists, who see the modern state as a primary contributor and not as a possible solution to the problems they feel are paramount in our age. Some view the term security as too specific to warrant expanded employment, others as too general to mean much subsequent to expansion.[27]

Since a subfield in the discipline of international relations or world politics styles itself as security studies, the term is an important one for social scientists engaged in this area. In the early 1990s, Barry Buzan called for an expansion of *security studies* (as autonomous from *strategic studies*, which focus more intensely on military matters) to include military, political, economic, and societal security. This still leaves us, of course, with somewhat nebulous categories; for example, Buzan defines environmental security as a concern with 'the maintenance of the local and planetary biosphere as the essential support system on which all other human enterprises depend.'[28] This leaves a great deal to interpretation, but at least makes clear the suggestion that the nation-state itself cannot be the end of analytic or normative thinking. Barring the invention and production of rather large biodomes, environmental security for one country only is a patently absurd idea. And to the extent that we are capable of some sort of universal application of human rights standards (prevention of state-induced death, and refugee protection rights, for two examples), such standards can't stop at borders either. Other authors have called for this type of a conceptual expansion, asserting that nonmilitary threats to national security deserve equal treatment; but they have done so without challenging the sacred nature of national security itself.[29]

Much of this 'meaning of security' is timely American introspection; and it is obvious that American support will be vital in forging the regulatory regimes needed to limit environmental degradation and, as problematically, to promote human rights in the future. The literature linking security with human rights questions and/or international environmental problems often calls for increased American assistance worldwide, to promote compliance with regulatory regimes and, in more directly political fashion, to promote 'democratization.' One can argue that this amounts to a summons for American universalism, and furthermore, that for such universalism to take root, the image of a frightening outside world must first be created.

Indeed, a standard approach has evolved, exemplified by Norman Myers, who looks at deforestation in the Philippines, water scarcity in the Middle East and Egypt, land degradation in El Salvador, and overpopulation in Mexico. First he explains what facet of American security is at risk; after this, he discusses these problems, neglecting their causal links with superpower security interests and American economic interests in general; he then ends by raising the spectre of Mexicans (three million of them) heading north into America should conditions in Mexico lead to violent revolution.[30] Myers's tactics are understandable: he knows that one markets products by appealing to insecurities.[31] Another example is *In the U.S. Interest*, an informative collection of essays edited by Janet Welsh Brown, which calls for greater development assistance to deal with environmental problems that affect American resource bases in the Southern Hemisphere.[32] At the very least, concerned analysts have called for increased multilateral diplomacy, or American 'leadership without primacy.'[33] The World Bank (indirectly controlled by Washington, according to many critics) is currently generating publications (the result of workshops and a financial infusion into the Bank's intelligentsia) that spell out the means for promoting democratization. This is as genuine a reflection as any of Washington's resolve to continue the bank's function as an agent spreading Western values around with a rather hot, well-buttered knife. We return to this theme in Chapter 5.

There is no absolute need, however, to adopt a maximalist definition of security simply because we are incorporating new threats into its meaning. Perhaps the most articulate of those promoting environmental security is Peter Gleick, who identifies four key environmental threats to security, all of which are relevant to resource studies: (1) Resource acquisition is in itself a strategic goal. (2) Resources are often attacked as part of military strategy. (3) Resources can be utilized as military tools ('ecosabotage' is gaining currency as a concept, but this category has equally sinister implications in the use of food and water as weapons). (4) Various disruptions to environmental services, such as water supply, are obvious threats to the well-being of citizens.[34] According to this perspective, we must view environmental threats within their proper context, as challenges to the national interest; and this invariably involves the participation of that organization whose explicated role in society is to protect that interest: the military establishment.

This is a serious problem for at least one analyst at the opposite end of the opinion spectrum, Daniel Deudney. He advises us to examine its temperament 'before harnessing the old horse of national security to pull the heavy new environmental wagon';

he feels that by viewing environmental security as a problem of the national interest, we risk sacrificing the world community approach to its solution.[35] Deudney argues that we should not worry about resource wars: today's trading system will provide ample resources; and it is increasingly difficult to exploit foreign resources through territorial conquest; and, finally, we live in the age of substitution, where 'industrial civilisation is increasingly capable of taking earth materials such as iron, aluminum, silicon and hydrocarbons (which are ubiquitous and plentiful) and fashioning them into virtually everything needed.'[36] In essence, however, Deudney's argument is about discourse. He asserts that treating environmental problems as security threats may subsume the former into mere categories of the latter. The world community must have priority. This is familiar phraseology: connections between global ecology and the need for world order have been made for some time, epitomized best perhaps in 1971 by Richard Falk's path-breaking *This Endangered Planet*, in which he asserted: 'A world of sovereign states is unable to cope with endangered-planet problems ... Such a system exhibits only a modest capacity for international cooperation and coordination. The distribution of power and authority, as well as the organization of human effort, is overwhelmingly guided by the selfish drives of nations.'[37]

No true-blooded realist would argue with the last point. But the focus of the argument around the merits of state sovereignty as an international institution has rarely been as sharp. The point is worthy of the repetition it has received in the literature: 'Because the solutions to the problems of the environment must be global they will present an unprecedented challenge to concepts of national sovereignty.'[38] So too will concerns over human rights, refugee status, and the rapid globalization many either welcome or despair of today.

Robert Walker questions the primacy of the state in our thinking about security. As a process wherein the 'principle of hierarchical subordination gradually gave way to the principle of spatial exclusion,' the historical development of the nation-state system produced the principle of state sovereignty, which, by

'offering both a spatial and a temporal resolution of the relationship between universality and particularity ... affirms a specific
account of who we are – citizens of particular states who have
the potential to work toward universal standards of conduct by
participating in statist political communities – and denies the
possibility of any other alternative."[39]

Perhaps that other alternative, necessarily vague, is a mix-
ture[40] of local identity and global consciousness – that is, a movement toward prioritizing environmental and human security on
both levels – and is represented by the work of nonstate actors
in the process.[41] Envisioning community on these coterminous
levels is indeed difficult. But without the customary trappings
of the state's monopoly on violence, it too may be hard to
imagine.

There is also the claim that security has been conceived from a
European point of view as the Westphalian system has gradually – and in many places rapidly – been imposed on the rest of
the world.[42] We will return to this argument in our chapter on
globalization, but a few points can be offered here. Timothy
Shaw argues that security should be viewed in an unconventional manner outside the traditional Eurocentric framework,
since it 'is inseparable from questions of the survival of states,
classes, factions and property: the "corporatist" nexus.'[43] This is
certainly a valid point, since the violence that disrupts civilian
life and creates such ecological and economic havoc in Africa
takes the shape of overt class, ethnic, and racial warfare conducted by state oppression and guerilla revolution. Of course,
this perspective opens a can of rather hungry worms, since it not
only changes the focus of security questions from the state to
groups or classes – which transcend national divisions themselves – but leads us inexorably to questions concerning state
legitimacy (and, in the Gramscian sense, hegemony), relations
between state and society (embeddedness, autonomy, and so
on), and the internal and external dimensions of national security. These questions are not usually encountered in security
analysts' theoretical inventories. But it is worth quoting Ken
Booth, whose reflective critique of contemporary security

studies ruffled a few feathers in the late 1970s: 'The prevailing Eurocentric definition of war results in our overlooking a considerable amount of human violence ... If we ignore the multitude of lesser conflicts which take place, we will underestimate the extent of social conflict throughout the world, and so tend to exaggerate the degree of order which exists.'[44]

This statement makes as much sense now, with the global bipolar conflict between East and West largely behind us, as it did then. If we are to understand contemporary human security problems, we must look beyond state–state violence. A minimalist interpretation of genocide, discussed in the next chapter, forces us to do just that, and it's high time international relations scholars did so. The refugee crisis, however, offers evidence that a state–state security outlook is far from obsolete, since it quickly becomes apparent that governments continue to defend borders from aliens, and often engage in multilateral efforts to do so.

One thing is certain: if an expanded concept of security is to be more than an empty rhetorical hull, it must promote analyses of those contemporary insecurities which affect us all, as individuals and as part of a global ecosystem. This is a tall order indeed. But by exploring the meaning of several prominent terms in global politics today, we may come closer to understanding what security can and cannot mean in the contemporary era. I have chosen four terms which I believe can force us to reconsider the burning global security questions of our time. I hope this effort will encourage readers to approach still other concepts with renewed vigour.

Conclusion

Today ... people ... feel policymakers may be unduly concerned with the 'interest of all mankind.' They see them sacrificing the less inclusive national community to the wider but in their opinion chimeric world community. The issue, then, is not one of transcending narrow group selfishness, as it was [in the 1930s], but rather one of according more exclusive devotion to the narrower cause of the national self.

Arnold Wolfers (1952)[45]

Rajni Kothari, an Indian scholar not prone to understatement, believes that the 'problematique of the human condition at the present juncture of world history [is] survival.'[46] On the personal level, we are all at least partially preoccupied with the quest for existential survival, and security is that which permits it. This is as close to a universal as we can get. The problem – the ambiguity, the confusion, the divide – begins as we discuss the security of aggregates and try to arrive at an operational definition of collectivities. Kothari accepts a rather sweeping one, 'the human condition,' while most political actors in international affairs are constrained by what Wolfers, in quite another era, called the 'less inclusive national community.' This ontological difference will permeate the grander academic discussions about defining security in world politics.

This is a good thing, for it throws into sharp relief two contrasting visions of a global future. Those who argue that such a polemical distinction between national and world security is either misleading or, since policy decisions are bound to reflect the former, irrelevant, put the idea of global society on false trial. For example, the move toward environmental sustainability will be an excruciating process for anxious environmentalists, involving the release of many predispositions and cultural attitudes held firm since the days of the original Enlightenment; patience is a cardinal virtue in terms of major change in world politics. If international society is in fact engaged in a cognitive process of adaptation – one that affects public, private, and personal sectors – it is a slow process, and profound optimism is unjustifiable.[47] Similarly, as Jack Donnelly and others remind us, even if we can achieve a universal acceptance of some standard of human rights (despite the Universal Declaration of Human Rights, we are without one), we will have to wait for states to comply with it, and there is little evidence on which we might base hope for this.[48] Even the Canadian government, which is quite vocal in the human rights area, is often criticized for placing trade considerations (self-gain) above human rights.

It is not difficult to explain why environmental security is vital. The key to the survival of any species, providing it is not being hunted directly by an overwhelming force, is habitat. This is elementary, and yet its praxiological corollary – that in order to provide for our survival, we must protect our habitat – is among the most divisive and confusing of aphorisms, and one whose relevance has been diminished by the quest of Western culture to separate itself from nature. In the age of the nation-state as the organizing principle of humanity, habitat has been replaced by territory, which in turn is defined by the existence of an outside world complete with real or potential enemies. The need for environmental security, and for its correspondence to some image of community, is perhaps much less controversial to the more recently colonized world. Especially less so to those peoples currently threatened with physical and cultural extinction by anthropogenic habitat destruction, such as the Yanomamo Indians of Amazonia, who fought among themselves for generations but now face a common outside threat. Or the Saami people in Arctic Fenno Scandia, who lost much of their livelihood because the Chernobyl meltdown raised the radioactivity levels of their reindeer to unacceptable levels.[49] Or the Pitjantjatjaran Aborigines in South Australia, displaced due to British nuclear tests conducted from 1953 to 1963.[50] And it is equally obvious that these people need to be respected as human beings with rights equal to those enjoyed by all of us, or else they will never achieve anything roughly resembling security at the group or individual level.

Of course, we all face the ultimate threat to sustainable life on earth presented by nuclear weapons, ozone layer depletion, and global climate change. In this light, the terms *sustainability* and *security* should be interchangeable. The debate over whether to accept environmental issues into the cherished circle of national security concerns should not be reduced to a polemical dispute between environmental activists and military nationalists. The nation-state is not going to crumble; and governments, influenced by ruling élites, will continue to exercise the vast majority of formal political power in the world. I'm not on a precarious limb predicting this. The danger is that the earth will crumble around the state; and that in this process anachronistic institutions will be unable to cope with this calamity, and may even be driven to genocidal policies to maintain power, as one might suggest occurred in Rwanda in 1994 (see Chapter Two). So we are left stuck with the state, yet in need of looking beyond it, which is a difficult position.

Quite difficult, because, as we will see in our discussions of genocide, ecocide, and refugees, state actors are so often complicit in the factors that give rise to these problems that any approach which does not at least challenge the state as primary actor begs the initial question of what really can be done. Amnesty International's Secretary General, Pierre Sane, described the 1994 United Nations Conference on Human Rights, held in Vienna, as a 'week of shame. The people who have the torturers and the killers on their payroll are here in Vienna mouthing phrases about human rights, and there is no evidence these diplomats have given a single order to stop ongoing torture, disappearances, political arrests or killings.'[51] Lothar Brock worries that, in the worst case, 'the concept of environmental security ... may be invoked to defend the status quo of the present world ecological order.'[52] Such concerns are common, and remind one of Richard Ashley's insistence that 'research and theory-building [should] avoid complicity in the very processes that contribute to the recurrence of violence and the pervasiveness of insecurity.'[53] Nonetheless, we might also acknowledge the hope in the voice of the late R.J. Vincent, who insisted that 'if the transnational recognition of subsistence rights improves the quality of government within states, we might extend a cautious welcome both to the penetration of the state and to its strengthening itself in response.'[54]

The debate over defining security can take on normative implications quite beyond the realm of everyday political analysis. For example, there was the 1960s World Order Models Project, which dared to be explicitly normative despite the prevailing bias against this sort of work at the time. Mel Gurtov, whom we discuss in our chapter on refugees, provides a recent and readable example of such work, insisting that bad values stand in the way of a more harmonious, equitable world. 'Global humanist' values include co-operation, spirituality, 'enoughness,' community, and personal growth; while realist and what Gurtov calls 'global-corporatist' values include such undesirables as competition, materialism, quantity, individualism, and the will to power.[55] The implication is that we will find true security only by adopting the former set. Gurtov's global humanism, with its accent on values, may strike one as an overly prudent approach to prescription, but it is – like most of the 'world order' literature – prompted 'by both idealism and a hard-headed political-economic concern about *structural violence.*'[56] Similarly, philosopher John McMurtry has written a fascinating critique of the dominant values inherent in the global market system – a theme to which we return in Chapter 5.[57]

Though perhaps less ambitious, many textbooks in this field follow a similar approach. A typical example is the highly readable collaboration by Janet Brown and Gareth Porter. They begin at the level of regime analysis but, thankfully, delve deeper and examine relevant structural and normative aspects: trade patterns, consumption habits, social paradigms, transnational class alliances, militarism, and so on.[58] This is the knowledge that Buzan's expanded security studies program, mentioned earlier, has a mandate to transmit. It also allows us to explore the implications of *mutual vulnerability* in a globalized economy, as Jorge Nef does in a recent monograph, and as we will in Chapter Five.[59]

Finally, even a global conception of security must have some limits. Humanity has a long history of solving problems by destroying them, and any conception of the environment that defines it as an impediment to human progress is bound to result in a similar reflexive mode. Many ecologists and political analysts alike have subscribed to Malthusian notions about the eventual overcrowding of the earth, or (less dramatically) to fears that population increases are leading inexorably to resource and wildlife depletion. While these fears are undeniably justified, we might take issue with some of the less thoughtful conclusions they put in play. For example, some of the more militant proponents of the 'Gaia hypothesis,' who view the world as a single living and semiconscious organism, believe that modern plagues such as AIDS, and mass famines in Africa, are simply Gaia's way of defending herself from overpopulation (if so, she would certainly choose more harmful humans to cull). The same can be said with regard to the effects of war. Malcome Brown, a senior *New York Times* correspondent who has seen the ecological effects of warfare (or what we term ecocide in Chapter 3) first hand, concludes: 'I have a feeling that if some intelligent panda could evaluate the real menace posed by the human race to other species, he might wish for more war, rather than less. From the non-human standpoint war at least has the merit of slightly slowing the human population explosion, the most devastating event in the planet's history.'[60]

Leaving aside the complex question of panda intelligence, it is difficult to see where this rhetoric takes us. We are, as the saying goes, in the stew together. In the end, of course, this is what we must come to terms with.

Ultimately, this book aims to display the inherent complexity of terminology as well as discuss some of the gravest and most frustrating problems facing humanity at this stage in time. Again, though the minimalist variations are, with one very significant exception, endorsed as most useful in social science, the last thing I would want to be accused of was attempting to establish or even contributing to the establishment of any new conceptual orthodoxies. In terminology, as in world politics, a certain element of anarchy is as inevitable as it is fascinating.

2

State Violence: Genocide[1]

genocide: *n.* deliberate extermination of a people or nation; genocidal *a.* [Gk *genos* race, -CIDE]

The Oxford Dictionary of Current English (1986), 308

We begin our terminological exploration with what is arguably the most painful concept of all. Unfortunately, it may also be one of the most reflective: future historians seeking an accurate theme for this fast-closing century might suitably adopt 'the age of genocide.' Despite unprecedented advances in communications, the rise of economic interdependence, and a half-century of the United Nations, we can still reflect on an era in which mass murder has been a frequently exercised state policy. The list of victims seems endless: Armenians, Ukrainians, Jews, Gypsies, East Timorans, Biafrans, Cambodians, Kurds, Bosnian Muslims, Tutsis, and Hutus. And these are only some of the ethnic categories of victims. One could add indigenous peoples, whose survival continues to be threatened by the destruction of their habitat and culture; and the millions of citizens who have been eliminated by paranoid governments and warring states. There are also those who have died prematurely due to starvation in a world capable of feeding us all, or due to environmental contamination.

Recently the United Nations has helped establish two International Criminal Tribunals, one for the former Yugoslavia and the other for Rwanda. In 1998 a permanent international court was established (in principle) that will have the jurisdiction to try those accused of genocide. And in a highly publicized case, the British government has detained former Chilean dictator Augusto Pinochet, at the request of a prosecutor in Spain, which hopes to extradite him to face charges of crimes against humanity and genocide. (Under his rule in the 1970s, some 3,000 Spanish citizens were killed in the name of Chile's 'national security.') The renewed popularity of the term *genocide* is indicative of the perseverence of state violence around the globe.

In the spring and summer of 1994, an outbreak of carnage in Rwanda shocked the Western world with images of dismemberment, displacement, starvation, and bloated corpses floating down the Kagera River into Uganda and Lake Victoria. In just two months of intense violence, half a million unarmed civilians were murdered.[2] It is believed that state-employed Hutu militias were responsible for much of the killing, which began after Hutu president Juvenal Habyarimana was killed in a rocket attack on his plane. Rwanda had been plagued with violence even before it achieved independence from Belgium in 1962. Indeed, it was a massacre of Tutsis in 1959 that created an exiled Tutsi community in Uganda, remnants of which returned to Rwanda in 1994 with the Rwanda Patriotic Front, which presently governs that country. But nothing in known African history has equalled the recent bloodbath in terms of its scope and – as chilling – the speed with which events took shape.[3] Since the genocide, efforts at administering justice have faced enormous hurdles, from an inhumanely crowded prison population to claims of atrocities committed by Tutsi government forces.

For a proper perspective on this century historians will of course look far beyond Africa. The Holocaust is still considered the supreme example of genocide. Estimates vary, but at least six million Jews were killed during it, and many others as well, including Gypsies, prisoners of war, and German 'undesirables,' such as disabled people and homosexuals.[4] Because of the massive numbers involved, and the administrative efficiency with which it was carried out, the Holocaust remains a singular event in history, though (as we discuss below) this singularity is debatable in sociological terms. In what many regard as a sad repetition of history, 'ethnic cleansing' campaigns have added to the misery of the splintered state of Bosnia. A ceasefire supported by NATO troops has ended the bloody civil war there; meanwhile, open conflict continues in other areas of the former Yugoslavia, such as Kosovo. Investigators are still uncovering evidence of mass murders committed by all sides during the Bosnian conflict. For all the optimism surrounding the fiftieth-year celebrations of the birth of the United Nations, a cruel cycle of violence seems to be in place in many parts of the world. Even Rwanda's gruesome river scenes are not new: Andrew Bell-Fialkoff informs us that during the Croatian/Nazi slaughter of Serbs, Gypsies, and Jews in 1941, 'so many corpses were thrown into the Danube ... that German authorities were forced to close the river to swimming.'[5]

Genocide can also be understood as referring to loss of life arising from state negligence or (even more broadly) from the disinterest of the world community. This conceptual position (which is the *maximalist* one in terms of this book) is often taken by those concerned about human rights in a more general sense than is permitted by a strict reading of *The Convention on the Prevention and Punishment of the Crime of Genocide* (1948). It is considered too broad an application of the term by some international legal experts; but others would argue that we must recognize those who are struggling for basic human needs – especially in the developing world – as the largest constituency of victims of genocide in this century. UN specialized agencies help promote awareness of how the world system has been structured in a manner that encourages rather than curbs these people's destruction.[6] Genocide, then, is not just about state terror, though any definition would of course include that phenomenon; it is also about high child mortality, the elimination of cultural differences by the spread of modernity, the destruction of the environment, and a host of other threats to life. In short, genocide is the extreme opposite of human and global security. In this chapter we will examine this terrible concept, in part by contrasting this broadened definition with the more limited legal one; we will then discuss some institutional implications for modern international organization.

Two related themes will emerge from the ensuing discussion: that of sovereignty, and that of justice. Leaving aside the important debate about the meaning and extent of modern sovereignty, one need not be a dedicated adherent to the *realist perspective* in world politics theory to admit its centrality.[7] At least with regard to its military implications, the principle of nonintervention is taken seriously by decision makers; any discussion of international or unilateral interventions designed to stop or prevent genocide, however it is defined, must struggle with this reality. Some would even argue that state sovereignty actually *facilitates* state violence; it is states, after all, that commit or at least encourage such large-scale atrocities. The theme of justice also posits a strong challenge to the international community when it comes to the particularly messy question of how to punish those who carry out genocide, again regardless of how we define the act. Rwanda's newest president, Pasteur Bizimungu, punctuated his address to the General Assembly by urging the speedy establishment of an international tribunal in order to help his government 'bring the culprits to justice.'[8] The international system is not designed for this task, though isolated and problematic attempts have developed to carry it out. And the maximalist conception of genocide produces a correspondingly expanded demand for justice.

Coupled with these conceptual concerns is, then, a more directly institutional dilemma. Given the foundation upon which the UN was constructed – as an alliance against the Axis war campaigns, which were accompanied by mass murder – we might demand to know why genocide is allowed to occur despite the UN's survival as an institution. *Liberal institutionalists* tend to point to the potential of what some scholars have termed *global prohibition regimes*: members are guided by norms that 'strictly circumscribe the conditions under which states can participate in and authorize [certain] activities and proscribe all involvement by nonstate actors.'[9] Thus slavery and piracy, though both occur in some areas of the globe even today, are internationally proscribed, as of course is genocide (at least in its minimalist conception, discussed below). Less success can be found in other areas, such as the eradication of poverty and the proliferation of conventional weapons of war (though a limited ban on land mines has evolved).

Institutionalism suggests that the solution to these problems, and arguably the problem of recurrent genocide, is the construction of avenues of regularity – the 'co-operation without coercion' that international organization facilitates. The UN remains the logical political space to accomplish this. With all due respect for the outraged cries for immediate humanitarian intervention that follow the outbreak of military hostilities that could be interpreted as genocidal, both sovereignty and justice demand an impartial UN, and a strong humanitarian orientation and not a military one is the most appropriate. This responsive role offers some resistance to both forms of genocide discussed later, while taking into account the limits of international organization in today's world system.

In summary, this chapter will explore two related questions, both of them with conceptual and institutional implications. Should the prevalent definition of genocide be changed to reflect an expanded scope of human rights concerns? And can justice in such matters be achieved while sovereignty remains the primary ordering principle of the nation-state system?

Contending Conceptions

There is much in a word, especially one as connotative as genocide, which from any standpoint signifies an event involving death and human suffering. This has immediate and public policy implications, as the Rwandan case demonstrated: according to one report, during late May of 1994, when the killings had reached a frenzied peak and over 500,000 Tutsis and moderate Hutus had probably been massacred, 'the U.S. Government had instructed its spokesmen not to label the deaths in Rwanda genocide, since doing so would have made it more difficult to stand aside and watch the slaughter continue.'[10] Of course, the word isn't always hidden from public view; it can be used for specific political purposes as well. For example, the Reagan Administration labelled the evacuation of villages on the upper Coco River in Nicaragua by the Sandinista government an incident of 'genocide.' Though the resettlement was indeed forced and involved the abuse of an indigenous population (the Miskito Indians), it did not involve the mass slaughter we usually associate with the term.[11] However, this example is indeed an exception. The word seems to act as psychological barrier, and once we have passed it, increased attention is almost demanded of us. In this light, genocide is usually recognized as the ultimate crime against humanity.

The word *genocide* was coined by Polish jurist Raphael Lemkin during the implementation of Hitler's Final Solution. Lemkin was deeply aware of the atrocities being committed across Europe, which were being carried out largely on racial grounds and which were affecting one ethnic group in particular, the European Jewish community. Thus he introduced a new term 'to denote an old practice in its modern development,' derived from the Greek word for race or people, *genos*, and the Latin *caedere* (cide), which means to kill.[12] Although born from the Holocaust experience, the term has grown as a concept with the passage of time and the persistence of atrocities. Indeed, for many its meaning has become much too broad. Fifty years after the Second World War, what does genocide mean today? As discussed in the preceding chapter, one can place the word on continuum. The *minimalist* definition centres on what is now the conventional understanding, forged from the Nuremburg Trials' condemnation of 'crimes against humanity'; the *maximalist* conception greatly expands this to include deaths caused by state negligence, imperial expansion, economic exploitation, and cultural destruction – factors to which we will return in our chapter on globalization.

The minimalist conception centres explicitly on *The Convention on the Prevention and Punishment of the Crime of Genocide*, which was the result of worldwide condemnation of the Nazi

Holocaust (1939–45). Some argue that the term should be reserved solely for that historical event, though this is an increasingly rare position.[13] The UN first used the word in General Assembly Resolution 96(I), of 11 December 1946, which was titled *The Crime of Genocide*, and which was the result of a request put forward by the Cuban, Indian, and Panamanian delegations. Interestingly, the UN Secretariat had originally drafted a convention that 'subsumed under "genocide" such acts as destroying the specific characteristics of groups by destroying their shrines, the confiscation of their property, the deprivation of their means of livelihood, the prohibition of their language, [and] the destruction of their books.'[14]

In the end, a narrower definition, which remains standing today, was accepted. The actual Convention – Resolution 260 (III) of 9 December 1948 – defines genocide as any of the following acts committed with 'intent to destroy, in whole or in part, a national, ethnic, racial, or religious group as such': 'a) killing members of the group; b) causing bodily harm or mental harm to members of the group; c) deliberately inflicting on the group conditions of life calculated to bring about its physical destruction in whole or in part; d) imposing measures intended to prevent birth[15] within the group; e) forcibly transferring children of the group to another group.'[16]

The Convention makes it clear that this is a crime in times of war *or* peace, and that a state's actions toward its own citizens could be considered a breach of *international* law. As well, genocide may be committed against people in states other than the one most concerned; this implies not only that states will be the main perpetrators, but also that certain war crimes committed under occupation may be viewed as genocide. The Convention also mentions the following as punishable: conspiracy to commit genocide, direct and public incitement to commit genocide, attempt to commit genocide, and complicity in genocide (the last point is no doubt a reference to Holocaust collaborators in occupied states during the war).[17] As for the (unspecified) punishment that a genocidal leader could expect, such decision was the responsibility of the state on whose territory the crime was committed, until such time as an international criminal court was established. This preserved the legal principle of territorial jurisdiction, as well as the political one of nonintervention. Article VIII gives contracting parties the right to call upon organs of the UN to take appropriate measures to prevent and suppress acts of genocide.[18] Perhaps *because of* its limitations, the Convention has been ratified (with various qualifications) by over one hundred states, including, after decades of reluctance, the United States. In 1998, delegates to a conference in Rome voted to establish a permanent international criminal tribunal, though many key states have refused to sign the final agreement.

Given the centrality of the doctrine of racial superiority in Nazi ideology, the Convention's explicit emphasis on ethnic identity and groups is understandable. Even so, it is often cited as a limitation. This became noticeable when, for example, it was claimed that Pol Pot could not be charged with genocide since his Khmer Rouge forces were not targeting a specific ethnic or racial group.The Khmer Rouge campaign in Cambodia, which claimed well over one million lives, was popularly termed 'autogenocide.' Alain Destexhe does not see 'what took place in the Cambodian killing fields' as a true genocide; that being said, he deeply resents the label 'autogenocide [which] suggests that the victims actually killed themselves and succeeds only in ... detracting from the guilt of those responsible.'[19] Similarly, Idi Amin, who is still enjoying a comfortable exile in Saudi Arabian, was said to have been nongenocidal because the majority of his victims were political and not racial enemies. Even the Rwandan massacre can be interpreted as a largely political event, since many 'moderate Hutus' were also killed. This does little to remove the fitting label of genocidal on the now disposed Hutu regime; it does, however, help dispel the quaint Western notion that such conflicts are but 'tribal' squabbles.

Though the Convention clearly makes it possible to charge individuals, including nonstate actors, with genocide, one thing is fairly certain: despite the Convention's political inability to articulate this, the cold logistics of genocide suggest the presence of the state, since few other organized groups could have the apparatus necessary to carry out the crime; and since governments have leaders, regardless of their particular hierarchy, those at the top must be the chief criminals. The Nuremburg Trials (which admittedly were a clear case of 'victor's justice') were quite explicit in establishing the precedent that the defence of 'following orders' must not be available to those charged with crimes against humanity: individuals must be held accountable (though the newly established Criminal Tribunal is less adamant on this issue). Yet – and here we begin to move away from a narrow, criminal definition of genocide – sociological theory has challenged the conventional notion that the intent of individual murderers is the sole cause of genocide. Helen Fein argues strongly that genocide must be conceived as 'organized state murder.'[20]

Somewhat ironically, this perspective shift was brought on partially by those who sought to explain the Holocaust by going beyond the *intentionalist* approach, in which 'the dictum of the singularity of Nazism correlates with the assumed singularity of the mindset of the main historical actors.'[21] Their alternative, which is to concentrate on the bureaucratic inevitability of the Holocaust, 'implicitly undermines the notion of the Holocaust's radical singularity and raises questions about destructive potentials in today's modern societies.'[22] The state, and by extension society, becomes the centre of complicity. Or, as sociologist Zygmunt Bauman suggests, the greatest 'terror permeating our collective memory of the Holocaust is the growing suspicion that [it] could be more than an aberration, more than a deviation from an otherwise straight path of progress ... that, in short, the Holocaust was not an antithesis of modern civilization and everything ... it stands for.'[23] This inevitably moves us away from the relative simplicity of the Convention, which was designed to facilitate the punishment of and ultimately deter murderous individuals, not states, nor for that matter complicit social structures and relations.

The advent of the nuclear age has taken us further toward an alternative and expanded perspective on genocide. It can be argued that nuclear deterrence was based on the threat of mass annihilation – the ultimate genocidal policy. Of course, one might argue that the threat of nuclear war in fact introduced a brand-new concept to the lexicon: *omnicide*. However, nuclear strategy was predicated upon the destruction of a specific enemy, and in that sense omnicide was not specifically intended (though it did not take much foresight to predict that it would result). It is this element of intention, or even incitement, that can lead to the nuclear arms race being labelled as genocidal. If, as UN officials have recently insisted, we can consider the Rwandan slaughter an instance of genocide because, for example, a Hutu official had given a speech in 1992 in which he 'explicitly called on Hutus to kill Tutsis and dump their bodies in the rivers,'[24] then what can we make of a system of national defence that called on thousands of soldiers to take part, if necessary, in the complete annihilation of hundreds of millions of civilians? Or does international (as opposed to civil) war justify such a technique? While the Hague Convention[25] merely states that the 'right of belligerents to adopt means of injuring the enemy is not unlimited,' it is certainly difficult to argue that the use of hydrogen bombs would be limited in any real manner.[26]

Such concerns move us toward the *maximalist* conception of genocide. The state remains pivotal: in many cases, what is often labelled 'state terrorism' (coercive violence perpetrated by states, be it against citizens of that state or of others) is viewed as genocide. State murder can take many forms. The deliberate starvation of entire communities, and the use of food as a weapon in general; the destruction of East Timor by the Indonesian military, or of Tibet by the Chinese, or of parts of Indochina by the Americans, or of political opponents by various Soviet regimes; or the draining of marshes in southern Iraq: all these cases involve mass death inflicted with obvious intent. By such an expanded definition, war is inherently genocidal. Cultural destruction that has a physical component, commonly called *ethnocide*, is a type of genocide; and so are the construction of large-scale dams that displace millions of people, deforestation that causes floods, and other forms of *ecocide* (see the next chapter for an expanded discussion).

The list cannot end here. Female infanticide in countries such as India and China may be viewed as a form of genocide over time. The reluctance of some Asian and African governments to respond to the health needs of AIDS patients could be viewed as genocidal. Noam Chomsky refers to American coercive trading in the tobacco sector, and warns of the 'blurring of the boundary between narcotrafficking and genocide.'[27] The use of poor minorities as front-line troops to fight wars, as was done by the Americans in Vietnam, is genocide, since it targets a specific group for what is at least the very high risk of being killed. The millions of children who die each year from simple diseases such as measles, pneumonia, and diarrhea can be seen as victims of 'silent genocide' – a term coined by World Health Organization director general Hiroshi Nakajima in reference to a WHO report indicating that roughly 11 million children die each year from easily preventable diseases. In the same vein, Henry Shue writes of the 'Holocaust of Neglect.'[28]

Likewise it could be claimed that the colonization of the 'New World' – a process called imperialism by some and progress by others – was in fact a genocidal process, and one which continues today. This leads to interesting alternative interpretations of the Convention and of state responsibility. For example, in October 1992 the International Tribunal of Indigenous Peoples and Oppressed Nations in the USA unanimously found the U.S. government guilty of numerous violations of international law, including the 1948 Genocide Convention.[29] More broadly, the modern nation-state, which demands a certain level of assimilation, could be seen as a genocidal machine. As one commentator suggests, 'the fiction of the nation-state is seldom innocuous. It often contains a prescription for the cultural destruction of a people through state policies of more or less compulsory assimilation and, at the limit, for genocide.'[30] By extension, then, the system that supports the nation-state as the primary political unit could be seen as a genocidal accomplice. Leo Kuper, commenting on the related principle of nonintervention, writes that 'the sovereign territorial state claims, as an integral part of its sovereignty, the right to commit genocide ... and the United

Nations, for all practical purposes, defends this right.'[31] If the state is the heart of the problem, any talk of humane intervention is tinged with hypocrisy.

So the list of possible instances (and culprits) of genocide appears endless. This is precisely the problem, minimalists will argue: a maximalist conception blurs the lines between genocide, aggression, violence, suffering, and other bad things. Alain Destexhe insists that 'there is a difference between a civilian killed in an air raid or from cholera in a refugee camp and one deliberately chosen for death on the grounds of being born a Jew or a Tutsi.' For him, only the Armenian massacre by the Young Turks of the Ottoman Empire (1915–16), the Holocaust, and the recent Rwandan carnage qualify as true cases of genocide.[32] While this is an extreme position, the minimalists do have a point. The difficulty with relating the maximalist definition to the Convention is that the latter includes the problematic terms 'deliberately' and 'calculated.' This means that in the case of high child mortality in the South or inner-city gunslayings in the North, one must assume these outcomes are the intended result of a planned policy by others, specifically the oppressors. This positivist element in identifying criminals clashes with sociological models of systematic infliction of suffering, or structural violence.

And it clashes with realistic political parameters as well. The case of war is a clear example. George Bush will not be charged with genocide, nor will the UN Gulf War Coalition. Yet acts such as bombing civilian areas in Iraq, and burying Iraqi soldiers alive, were certainly deliberate actions resulting in mass death. Urban carpet-bombing campaigns during the Second World War, which were conducted simultaneously with the Holocaust, were not on the agenda at Nuremburg or Tokyo. Arguments about means and ends aside, and moving beyond the simple 'the victors write history' cliché, this suggests that the minimalist and maximalist conceptions are actually quite far apart when it comes to under-standing what the world community *can* and *will* do about genocide; and perhaps the term does lose utility if it refers to a crime, or to an event defined by some as a crime, that cannot be punished. The 'silent genocide' that kills millions of malnourished children each year around the globe can hardly be explained with reference to one actor, and it can only be redressed through long-term development. To assert that the North, and the affluent, are complicit in this situation is one thing; to charge them with outright genocide raises several unanswerable questions.

Though the term genocide will continue to be used for its emotive power, and will remain highly subjective, I will suggest here that we need to take both conceptualizations into account. The maximalist no doubt sacrifices empirical focus, as well as legal redress in the more limited instance of direct, state-induced murder. Thus the late Raphael Lemkin would probably argue that we must not allow the concept of genocide to be eclipsed by that of 'human rights.' Regardless of one's preferred definition, the essential fact remains that genocides have been carried out throughout this century. Without being overly pessimistic, we may predict that they will occur again in the future, in both senses of the word. To maximalists, this may seem obvious; unfortunately, it may presently seem obvious even to minimalists.

Genocide, Sovereignty, and Justice

We are faced with two unavoidable themes: sovereignty as an institution, and justice as a fundamental concern in world politics. The sovereignty question remains central in the debate over what to do about genocide. The justice question is perhaps even more complicated, but both our definitions of genocide insist on the idea that injustice has occurred and that it must at some level meet with a response from the international community of sovereign states. Put together, the two themes provide some background regarding the very practical question of UN policy.

With regard to the institution of sovereignty, two immediate points can be made. The creation of states can be seen as a deterrent to genocide and a means of promoting ethnic rights. For example, the 'perceived need for Armenians and Jews to have respective territories ... to prevent future genocide is an obvious example of the reaction of a community which fears for its survival.'[33] In this light, sovereignty is protective and the state provides invaluable human security. Yet at the same time, sovereignty has legal implications, especially in connection with ruling élites, who enjoy freedom from external intervention even when they are inciting and committing genocide. As usual in world politics, we are dealing with a very sharp double-edged sword.

The realist perspective on world politics maintains the notion that, at least in the abstract, sovereignty is the defining feature of the world political system; and that international justice is thus contingent on an order based on sovereignty. Liberal institutionalists, on the other hand, believe that sovereignty is a diffuse concept, and one which must be viewed as one part of a larger network of interstate communication and regime formation; thus, justice is important within a corresponding 'conceptualization of progress in terms of human freedom and the importance attributed to liberal democracy, free trade, cognitive changes, communications, and moral norms.'[34] A core of liberal values permeates this perspective, which at least implies a sense of universal justice at the individual level – what Hedley Bull termed the 'Kantian or universalist view of international morality,' which demands a morality based on common humanity and not borders.[35] Still others tend to see sovereignty as a negative, as an oppressive institution that aids the wealthy or, in the less neomarxist sense, precludes genuine international harmony; to them, social injustice is a central issue that demands the focused attention of all who are engaged in the transformation of the global order.

Sovereignty affects the minimalist conception of genocide since, in the formal sense, the realists are right: sovereignty remains pivotal, manifested in (selective) adherence to the non-interventionary principle. As Kuper insists, states play the main role in genocidal activities, and the institution of sovereignty serves to perpetuate modern nation-states. However, we can accept the rather stretching idea that national sovereignty is solely responsible for the possibility of genocide *only if* we can cogently argue that its absence would result in a world that is free of genocide. Since genocide is typically carried out by governments, the absence of such political constructs might by definition preclude genocide. (This assumes further, of course, that whatever replaced the institution of Westphalian sovereignty did not itself promote mass killings – an uncertain assumption at best.) Still, one might assert that if states are the chief culprits, a perspective that does not adequately seek to explain the state, but is content to observe states at the level of their interaction, cannot contribute to an understanding of genocide.

Yet we can certainly ask ourselves why the international community fails to stop genocide. Surely the main reasons would include a reluctance to become engaged in messy campaigns of intervention that challenge the sanctity of sovereignty, and to commit significant forces to prolonged exposure to immediate danger. Costly interventions to prevent or stop genocide are rare, although some precedents exist, such as the French intervention in Lebanon in 1861, to protect Maronite Christians from persecution; the Russian, British, and French intervention to end atrocities in the Greco-Turkish war; India's effort to end atrocities by West Pakistani troops in Bangladesh in 1971; and Tanzania's invasion of Uganda (after Idi Amin had invaded Tanzania). Some might even include Operation Desert Storm, which forced Iraqi troops from Kuwait in 1991. However, all these cases involve greater issues and interests, and would not be seen as humanitarian operations by certain participants. One could argue that the effort to defeat Hitler, which was certainly not centred around saving the Jewish community, has been reinvented as a battle against genocide.[36]

Sovereignty affects the maximalist definition as well, since any attempt to deal with social injustice must involve nation-states or, to be more precise, governments. This is not to reduce the importance of the role played by nongovernmental organizations and community-based development initiatives. However, governments are the only organizations capable of dealing with modern humanitarian emergencies, and thus the development of related institutions that engage multilateral responses is vital. At the same time, there is little doubt that the international recognition given to extraordinarily oppressive regimes as sovereign entities reduces the chances that they will modify their behaviour as a result of rhetorical codemnation (in the age of economic globalization, regimes like Myanmar's SLORC continue to attract foreign capital). And it is even less likely that the dominant powers of the North will either receive or consider such condemnation themselves. How would Canadian officials respond to charges that Canada is in effect an apartheid state, and that the high suicide rates among its native people constitute a form of genocide? Again, the ambiguity of the maximalist position limits its utility.

With regard to the theme of justice, the minimalist focus is on punitive measures to enforce or promote the Convention. The persistence of sovereignty, it may be suggested, has made the pursuit of legal justice in this matter almost impossible, since the very perpetrators of the crime (states) are in essence immune from prosecution, though some individuals may eventually be punished during or after transition stages. The maximalist position focuses more on notions of entitlement. Here we ask the broader questions related to North–South or (more generally) rich–poor relations. At this point the discussion of justice blends into one of resource redistribution and, in the case of indigenous peoples, the right to self-determination. This is a much wider agenda. While the UN has developed a number of forums for dealing with such questions, from General Assembly discussions to high summitry to actual development policymaking and program implementation, that body is in constant financial peril and is often accused of inappropriate policymaking. The 'quiet' genocide recognized by the maximalists is a symptom of an unjust global order, which can be overcome only through a transformation quite beyond the isolated capability of states, or even regimes of states.

Of course, some people, less sanguine about the human prospect than liberal institutionalists, would suggest that in the long run, sovereignty and contemporary perspectives on justice are ephemeral. It is human nature, which is immutable, that leads inexorably to conflict and often violence; perhaps it is what led, sixty years ago, to the gates of Auschwitz. This fatalistic vision is best left for philosophers and theologians to debate. It is enough to say here that violence in any form is the result of moral relaxation, and that power and paranoia make a bad mix.

An Institutional Response?

What then of the United Nations, the primary international institution in world affairs? We should say at the outset that the UN is not by any means an autonomous body – it can do only what its members permit it to. While it is heartening that the *Convention on the Prevention and Punishment of the Crime of Genocide* has been overwhelmingly endorsed, putting even a dull set of teeth in the Convention has been another story. Barbara Huff believes that we need 'a recognition of the essential juridical truth that genocide transcends the interests of states and individuals. In other words, if genocide is a crime under international law, as all agree, then it is everyone's responsibility to impress upon policy makers the necessity to act upon violations of it.'[37] The tribunals that have been formed to bring war criminals from the Yugoslavian conflict to justice may turn out to be a first step toward this. It remains to be seen whether Bosnia, Kosovo, or Rwanda will provide sufficient impetus for the actual implementation of a permanent criminal tribunal with general jurisdiction.[38]

But what court could realistically deal with the Rwandan case? Rwanda's new prime minister, Faustin Twagiramungu, has stated that no less than 22,000 employees of the former government are suspected of complicity in the massacres of 1994, and that thousands more were part of the killing militias known as the Interahamwe. It is widely recognized that thousands more Hutu citizens killed their Tutsi neighbours and participated in mob killings – and this in a country whose court system is a shell of its former self. Some top Rwandan officials have been tried, though only because the former government lost a war. Beyond that, it is simply unrealistic to assume that all those involved in murders will be charged. What about all the Chetniks who participated in the genocidal rape campaign in Bosnia? The same will probably hold for the trials to take place in Ethiopia for crimes committed under Mengistu Haile Mariam's brutal rule. The 1979 'trial' and execution of the one-time president-for-life, Francisco Macias Nguema, hardly resolved things in Equatorial Guinea. Justice cannot be complete in such matters, and it will as often as not be part of the process whereby a new elite establishes its own moral legitimacy. The UN, however internationalist its ethos, will not escape the perception that it is simply aiding this process.

It is vital that the UN continues to play a role in the detection and, possibly, prevention of genocide. To do so it must remain as impartial as possible. The UN is required to obtain consent before engaging in peacekeeping for a good reason: as Somalia demonstrated, the belligerents will hardly go along with the UN if they feel it has taken sides. If a Chapter VII mandate were ever to be passed based on widespread condemnation of a government's actions, full-scale invasion to prevent or stop genocide would be justified by almost anyone's standards. This is a highly unlikely event, however. As well, the most immediate effect of violence is the displacing of those who are fleeing it; and here the UN and related NGOs are absolutely crucial. Humanitarian assistance must remain pivotal; and UN protection forces for safe havens, which will of course be messy, may be quite necessary. (The herculean efforts of the UN High Commissioner for Refugees should be matched with funding that at least *approaches* adequacy. We return to this theme in Chapter 4.)

However, the argument that the UN should become active in fighting civil wars is much less convincing.[39] One reason for this is that most civil wars that involve genocide would force the UN to fight directly against governments and on the side of rebels – an unlikely scenario, given the reluctance of member states to support this type of interference. Indeed, the opposite is quite possible: the UN could end up dedicated to preserving 'order' even when civil rebellion is justified. No disinterested omniscient force is available to determine the validity of interventions at the political level. Another reason a militarized UN is problematic is that, in any modern intervention, great losses can be expected, and this will further reduce the UN's ability to attract the personnel necessary to provide humanitarian relief (assuming it does not resort to hiring mercenaries). Over time, the UN cannot police such situations – a frustrating fact, and one that the fashionable zeal for rapid intervention obscures. From a foreign policy perspective, the cold, hard reality for decision makers is that armed interventions to stop genocide will require the public to accept the casualities that are sure to follow. The argument that a standing UN force would relieve politicians of this responsibility posits disturbing questions about its democratic legitimacy. No one believes that the UN is a truly democratic global organization that actually supersedes national governments on such matters. As an example, where is the outpouring of condemnation over what the Russian army has done recently in Chechnya?

Since some schemes for UN reform would create an armed force at its disposal, there is also the related question of whether it would be morally acceptable for the Secretary General or (a more likely scenario) the Security Council to give orders to engage in armed conflict. The recently established ad hoc international war crimes tribunals do not have the authority to impose the death penalty as punishment.[40] If those found guilty by international experts, after as fair a trial as possible, cannot be put to death on UN authority, then how can we justify giving the Secretary General, or the Security Council, the right to commit armed forces to open warfare – an act that would invariably involve imposing a death sentence on at least some of the participants in the conflict at hand? Furthermore, in the event that excessive force is used by these forces, could the UN legitimately put soldiers from participating states on trial?

Regarding the maximalist conception of genocide, the UN must continue to play a key role in alleviating poverty and, perhaps as importantly, setting an international agenda based on North–South relations. This will not overcome questions of state complicity in mass starvation and terrorism, nor will it fundamentally alter those structures which allow such infringements on human rights to occur. It will not in itself defeat militarism, or (as realists would quickly remind us) replace the foreign policy canon of national interest with a globalist perspective. Nor will it automatically diminish the ugliness of stark, brutal state power; or attempts to achieve and impose such power; or the shameful use of ethnicity and religion by political opportunists.

But to dismiss the UN because it cannot achieve these things is unfair. The complex web of human rights conventions and commissions and development agencies that the UN has fashioned over the years may be seen as part of a painfully evolving international society. As this century of genocide ends, we must look to such institutions for help in avoiding more of them. But we cannot overlook the possibility that there will be more genocides in the future. The lament of Idi Amin's successor, Godfrey Binaisa, will probably be heard again: 'For eight years [my people] cried out in the wilderness for help; unfortunately, their cries seemed to have fallen on deaf ears.'[41]

Finally, we might argue, with those whom Zacher and Matthews have termed 'Republican Liberals,'[42] that if the spread of democracy and of the rule of law can help us avoid international warfare, perhaps it can also reduce the use of genocide as state policy. Some adherents of the maximalist position would reject this out of hand, arguing that liberal democracies are implicit culprits in the suffering of the masses. But the minimalist perspective would be much more friendly, since whatever openness in government there may be will surely reduce the likelihood that such a government would commit the act of genocide as defined in the Convention. Here our two perspectives converge: the best way to ensure that sovereign states do not resort to genocide is to promote their inclusion in a universal, but necessarily limited, human rights agenda.

Conclusion

Should the conventional definition of genocide be changed?

Given the problems involved in assigning blame for genocide, and the need for an international Convention to which governments will at least pay lip service, the minimalist definition seems most appropriate. This in no way suggests that states should be exonerated from the contributions they make to the material discomfort of citizens; nor does it suggest that political repression itself should not be viewed with equal disdain. But there is a certain logic to the Convention that is thrown into semantic chaos by the maximalist perspective, even if the latter is more intellectually accommodative of an expanded vision of human rights in this century. Collective historical experiences such as chronic underdevelopment, the destruction of indigenous peoples, the Holocaust, and the threat of nuclear annihilation have stretched our understanding of what genocide can mean. But for the purposes of conceptual clarity, the word should be used with care.

Is the achievement of justice related to genocide possible in a world of sovereign states? The quick answer is negative. International tribunals have a symbolic value that is undeniable, and the Bosnian and Rwandan cases may set a precedent for their use; but at the same time they present many questions of legitimacy related to sentence enforcement and the spectre of victor's justice. This is not to suggest that war crimes, and crimes against humanity such as genocide and rape, should not be prosecuted by the international community, but rather that prosecution will be a troubled endeavour.

When it comes to humanitarian intervention, the UN must adhere to the increasingly hazy rule of impartiality. There is a strong need to monitor human rights and to watch for the signs of impending genocide: too often, ethnic hate campaigns, dehumanization tactics, expropriation of property, and massive population transfers. But the UN itself must resist militarization, which would crush any long-term legitimacy it hasn't already lost. This is perhaps the cruellest truth about genocide: too often it will not be stopped unless other states are willing to go to war to stop it, and quite frankly, in most cases they will not be.

Françoise J. Hampson, arguing for the establishment of war

crimes trials after the latest Gulf War (1990–91), suggested that we 'become accessories to crimes whose condemnation we do not secure owing to our own inaction.'[43] This is, of course, a moral position rather than a factual statement. But taken to a similar ethical conclusion, the maximalist version of genocide suggests that those who can help its victims but fail to do so are complicit in their victimization. The humanitarian impulse, which is under constant attack in the debt-strapped North, must be preserved through the multilateral institution of the UN. We must insist that this body engage in substantive measures to reduce strife and poverty, but there are limits to what can be done *by* the nation-state system *for* the nation-state system. In the end, nonstate and non-UN actors will play as important a role.

Finally, the formal split between the minimalist and maximalist perspectives of genocide, while an intellectually intriguing dichotomy, is of course less final than is suggested in this academic discussion. Ultimately, there are connections between the killing of specific groups as state policy, and the continuation of social injustices that have resulted in less direct but equally harmful human consequences. Genocide scholar Irving Horowitz believed in 1976 that, 'if candour is to prevail, statesmen and scholars alike would have to admit that the umbilical cord between genocidal practice and state power has never been stronger.'[44] Perhaps it is this old link that calls out for the most intense future exploration by both minimalists and maximalists.

We turn away now from this discussion of the destruction of human beings, and consider the destruction of the environment which sustains them.

3

Environmental Degradation: Ecocide[1]

eco-: *prefix* ecology, ecological (*ecoclimate*).[foll.]

-cide: *suffix* person or substance that kills (*regicide, insecticide*); killing (*homicide*).[L *caedo* kill]

Oxford Dictionary of Current English (1986), 232, 125

Our next term for investigation has maximalist and minimalist understandings as well, and though it is a less popular term than genocide, it is just as ominous. Criticisms of the American operations in the Vietnam war ushered the term *ecocide* into the lexicon of social science. In the context of American strategies in Indochina, which included defoliant (or, rather euphemistically, 'leaf abscission') and land-clearing programs designed to expose enemy cover, the term ecocide clearly referred to the destruction of ecological systems by deliberate force.[2] It was employed as a critical device as well as an analytic concept by a community of scholars opposed to such counterinsurgency policies. The term has been expanding since then, so that it now encompasses the economic forces that destroy rainforests and clog city highways and pollute mountain regions, as well as the less intentional effects of warfare on the environment – in particular, the threats to environmental security presented by nuclear weapons production and testing. As a conceptual term, ecocide has remained fashionable, but it has also lost any clarity it once enjoyed.

This chapter will continue our maximalist/minimalist framework with an examination of two understandings of ecocide, a term that has many links with security itself as an expanded post– Cold War concept. Analytic clarity demands that we separate the two conceptions and then re-evaluate the use of this rather strongly suggestive term. The first understanding perceives eco- cide as a strategy and consequence of militarism (both in warfare and, in a less widely accepted usage, in domestic national secu- rity activities). *Militarism* usually connotes excessive reliance on military means and methods; or, in the reflectivist sense, respect for military virtues such as loyalty to state and commander and discipline in the ranks. The second understanding is part of a crit- ical perspective on modern society and perhaps on *modernity* itself. It suggests that ecocide is an inherent aspect of industrial development and that militarism is but one facet of that historical process (here we see shades of both eco-anarchist and postmod- ernist literatures). Both conceptions have great merit but also present difficulties.

Most traditionally, ecocide has been viewed as a strategy that, in the heat of battle, becomes rather indistinguishable from a gen- ocidal campaign (in our minimalist sense of that term): it becomes an end in itself, one that is pursued with the steady application of modern technology. When the Iraqi military employed oil spills and fires during the 1990–91 Persian Gulf conflict, they high- lighted yet another dimension to ecocide as war: it may also be a deliberate strategy of distraction or desperation. We might con- sider this the more conventional definition, one that is almost synonymous with the term environmental warfare, though there are distinctions. On a policy level and from the perspective of *institutional response* (see the previous chapter on genocide), eco- cide should also be seen as one of the many problems encoun- tered by contemporary international law. A *Convention on the Prohibition of Military or Any Other Hostile Use of Environmental Modification Techniques* (ENMOD) was adopted in 1977, and the Additional Protocol I to the 1949 Geneva Conventions was also signed in 1977, but the Persian Gulf conflict is concrete evidence of the limited effectiveness of such agreements.[3]

But ecocide is now perceived as involving much more than direct warfare, and here we inch closer to a maximalist position. As a result of the arms race, which drove the nuclear powers to absurd heights of dependence on nuclear security, ecocide also came to be viewed as an unintended result of military strategy and preparation, and in particular one that harmed the local environmental security of those American and CIS citizens (many of them aboriginal peoples) who were unfortunate enough to be considered disposable for the cause of national security. It is important here to note the global nature of this process, which continues to this day as weapons plants are shut down and the true costs of the Cold War become clear. As Mike Davis writes in a recent essay, the environmental horrors of Chelyabinsk-40 and the Semipalatinsk Plygon (top-secret Soviet military production and testing sites) 'have their eerie counterparts in the poisoned, terminal landscapes of Marlboro County' (in the American Southwest).[4] The distinction between this and the *ecocide as war* concept may seem specious: Aren't both the result of the same social phenomenon, that is, militarism? This may be so, but it can be argued that the more significant link between these two understandings of ecocide – and there are real differences between them: one relates to intended effects while the other has much more to do with shameful negligence – is the question of the human rights of those who are affected, both in warfare and in peacetime, by military-related activities.

There is another understanding of ecocide as a concept, one that roughly reflects a maximalist position: it can be viewed as a broader process that takes place even in the absence of overt military warfare or preparation, and that has more to do with the ecological crisis affecting all people in all nations as we slide toward an increasingly uninhabitable world. In other words, the term has been used to describe the general effect of what we might, with appropriate trepidation, call the forces of modernity: industry, resource extraction, urbanization, chemical agriculture, and the oft-cited problems of overpopulation in the South and overconsumption in the North. This use of the term, which suggests that violence underlies the relations between humans and nature, informs much of the critical literature that emanates from ecofeminists and from those advocating post-materialist societies. In the same context, ecocide is a descriptive term, as is indicated by the title of one of the most influential books on environmental problems in recent years, which focuses on the environmental legacy of Stalin's Soviet Union.[5] The problem is that while the maximalist definition has interesting ramifications for the study of the nexus between environment and society (or, in a word, ecopolitics), the term in this context may be too broad to be useful. It also returns us to the issue that separates the first two faces of ecocide mentioned earlier – that of deliberate intent. Are we justified in viewing the history of a nation-state such as the U.S.S.R. – or for that matter of the entire globe – as a slow process of something called ecocide? Regardless of our answer, the term's broader definition offers interesting conceptual ground, as found for example in ecofeminist literature.

Before exploring these two understandings of the concept of ecocide, we must add an important caveat: there are many causal connections that one may draw between the relevant factors; but in this chapter, indeed in this entire book, we deliberately avoid making any linear causal routes seem preferable. For example, one might argue that the prevalent Western attitude toward nature facilitates militarism, which makes war possible if not inevitable. Or we might suggest that thousands of years of exposure to warfare have reduced humanity's capacity for natural stewardship or long-range perspective. By drawing these linkages, we come, as it were, full circle: the minimalist and maximalist conceptions meet. A later section of this chapter will address this question of circularity, which offers perhaps the most conceptually ambitious, if empirically limited, understanding of our topic. But this chapter, like others in the book, is merely a preliminary foray into this vast issue-area; we make no pretensions about offering a definitive theoretical contribution at this stage. We wish merely to compare two prevalent understandings of ecocide: one related to warfare and militarism as either strategy or consequence; and the other related to the ravages of industrial society. We will conclude that though both are of great heuristic value, the former has greater relevance to the study of environmental problems and social science.

The First Understanding

One of the least documented areas in the history of warfare is the environmental consequence of protracted military conflict. When it came to assessing the effects of war and war preparations, the environment was a geostrategic factor, but not one in its own right. Rather ironically, it was the advent of the nuclear age that began to change this. By considering the damage potential of nuclear weapons, scientists began to cast light on the harmful effects of nuclear war on ecosystems.

Perhaps the most widely read example of such Armageddon-like forecasting was Carl Sagan's discussion in *Foreign Affairs* of 'nuclear winter' – the climatic catastrophe – that might follow even a small-scale nuclear war. An earlier book on the same subject by Jonathan Schell was also widely read. Public awareness of the dangers of nuclear testing was partly responsible for the signing of the Partial Test Ban Treaty in 1963.[6] The debate over nuclear winter that followed Sagan's and others' work assumed familiar ideological lines, as Theodore Rueter and Thomas Kalil demonstrated in a review essay: 'Many hawkish and dovish strategic analysts strove (sometimes in bizarre fashion) to utilize nuclear winter as an argument for their previously held policy preferences. For hawks, nuclear winter was an additional argument for counterforce and limited nuclear options; for doves, it was an additional argument for disarmament and arms control.'[7]

More recently, the end of the Cold War and the deliberate burning of an estimated 500 million barrels of oil in Kuwait,[8] have provoked a shift away from preoccupations with nuclear weaponry and toward concerns over how conventional warfare has harmed ecosystems and caused related population displacements in various regions of the world. Most of the literature on nuclear weapons is based on conjecture; in contrast, evidence of the damage that conventional warfare inflicts is far more concrete. The damage inflicted on Indochina's forests by the American military, and especially by the U.S. Air Force, provided a ready focus for investigators in the early 1970s.[9] The Vietnam war coincided with a growing environmentalist movement in the United States, and was probably the first military campaign to be criticized heavily for its environmental impact. In a 1970 book featuring articles by Jean Paul Sartre, Orville Schell, Arthur Westing, Noam Chomsky, and others, Barry Weisberg, the volume's editor, defined ecocide as the 'premeditated assault of a nation and its resources against the individuals, culture and biological fabric of another country and its environs ... To understand the destruction of Indochina as ecocide requires that we come to understand that the ecosystem of Southeast Asia is one organic fabric in which all living things are tied together by an infinite number of interdependent strands.'[10]

Weisberg's definition makes three important points. *First*, ecocide is a 'premeditated assault'; it is purposeful environmental destruction.[11] *Second*, it is inflicted by one nation upon another (thus it is an international problem, not a domestic one). And *third*, it is so egregious because the various components of a given ecosystem are closely linked. You can't, in the tradition of reductionist science, employ 'surgical' ecocide – it's an all-or-nothing strategy. The definition serves as a foundational one. However, it is rather limited. For example, it is often difficult if not impossible to distinguish between the deliberate and the incidental effects of military strategies, as the following discussion will demonstrate. And we must, especially in the post–Cold War era in which civil wars are much more frequent than international ones, include cases where governments use ecocide against their own citizens or in which warring factions produce situations where environmental damage becomes a survival mechanism for the displaced. This being said, we will now discuss the empirical linkages between the environment and warfare.

Strategies and tactics, both offensive and defensive, by definition involve a good deal of environmental assault and modification. This is a truism as old as war itself. As early as 2400 B.C., Entemenar, the ruler of Sumer, modified the land by constructing a canal that diverted water from the Tigris to the Euphrates watershed; this ceased Sumer's dependence on the Kingdom of Umma. As Fred Roots has pointed out, the groundwater rose as a result of this construction, which caused rapid salinization, which impoverished Umma. Eventually, however, Sumer suffered as well, as its own overirrigated desert soils were leached. Roots concludes that by 2200 B.C., 'mighty Sumer was easy prey for upstart Babylon, which had less wealth and poorer technology but a clean environmental base.' A further note: Roots cites the most famous Biblical example of environmental modification for military purposes – the parting of the Red Sea by Moses: 'The mechanism by which Moses accomplished this rapid environmental modification is not clear to ordinary mortals today, but presumably he did it all by triggering tectonic movements. Certainly the geological structure and accumulated crustal stress in the Red Sea graben makes this a good potential location ... if God is on your side.'[12]

Arthur Westing, probably the most industrious author in the general field of environment/security linkages, has worked alone and with the Stockholm International Peace Research Institute and the United Nations Environmental Program.[13] He has compiled a list of ecologically disruptive wars, the earliest being the Persian-Scythian War of 512 B.C. (as the Scythians retreated they hindered Persian pursuit with a scorched-earth policy – a common theme in military history). The Peloponnesian War (431–404 B.C.), made famous by Thucydides, saw the annually repeated destruction of Athenian grain crops by the Spartans. At the end of the Third Punic War, the Roman victors polluted the farmland around Carthage with salt. Genghis Khan, leading the Mongols through Asia and eastern Europe, killed all unappropriated livestock and destroyed irrigation works located along the Tigris River in Mesopotamia. In the Franco-Dutch War of 1672–78, the Dutch flooded their own land to keep away French troops. The destruction of agricultural land, with the goal of starving rebel states into the Union, was routine policy during the last years of the American Civil War. The Chinese used scorched earth tactics to put down the Tai Ping revolt (1850–64). The Portuguese used herbicides to destroy crops during the Angolan War of Independence (1961–75). And the list goes on.[14]

In the more contemporary sense, localized ecosystem destruction, intended to flush out enemy forces in areas of high cover such as forests, marshes, and grasslands, and to deprive them of food supply, is best achieved by a narrow range of special-purpose weapons, especially chemical herbicides such as the infamous Agent Orange (2,4-D and 2,4,5-T), Agent White (2,4-D and Picloram), and Blue (cucodylic acid).[15] The use of such herbicides has generated understandable moral outrage in the United States.[16] In addition to the landscape alteration wrought by the infamous 'Rome plough,' more than 17 000 square kilometres of South Vietnam were damaged by herbicides, and over 1500 square kilometres of ecologically sensitive mangrove forest was completely destroyed.[17] The use of such techniques has long-term consequences. The German Army first used liquid chlorine – which inflames the lungs, causing those exposed to drown in their own exudation – near Ypres, Belgium, in April 1915. In June 1916, during the Battle of the Somme, the Allies used the even deadlier phosgene gas. According to Robert Harris and Jeremy Paxman, 'Long after the initial bombardment had occurred, an area which had been contaminated by mustard gas was liable to remain dangerous. The liquid formed pools in shell craters ... It polluted water. In cold weather it froze like water and stayed in the soil: mustard used in the winter of 1917 poisoned men in the spring of 1918 when the ground thawed.'[18]

It wasn't until Vietnam, however, that environmental warfare became feasible on a large scale. The American military attempted to use cloud-seeding technology to increase rainfall in the region; the point of this was to slow down enemy movements by inducing landslides along roadways and washing out river crossings.[19] According to one report, in 1969–70 the U.S. military actually tried to inflict a drought on Cuba. The idea here, according to Lawrence Juda, was to 'cause clouds to drop their rain before reaching Cuba thus causing a damaging drought.'[20] There is no doubt that the U.S. military had at least contemplated such weather modification in the past. The Vice-President of the U.S. Institute for Defense Analysis during the early and mid 1960s, geophysicist G.J.F. MacDonald, discussed such possibilities in a book published in 1968:

> One could ... imagine field commanders calling for local enhance-ment of precipitation to cover or impede various ground opera-tions ... We are presently uncertain about the effect of seeding on precipitation downwind from the seeded clouds, but continued seeding over a long stretch of dry land clearly could remove suffi-cient moisture to prevent rain 1000 miles downwind [which] leads to the possibility of covertly removing moisture from the atmosphere so that a nation dependent on water vapour crossing a competitor country could be subjected to years of drought. The operation could be concealed by the statistical irregularity of the atmosphere. A nation possessing superior technology in environ-mental manipulation could damage an adversary without reveal-ing its intent.[21]

The ambitions of military science are boundless. MacDonald added later: 'A controlled hurricane could be used to terrorize opponents over substantial parts of the populated world.' A con-trolled hurricane?

The results of climatological engineering are, at best, extremely difficult to measure: though there was heavy flooding in Vietnam in 1971, it is impossible to determine the exact cause. Critics of the Pentagon must have winced when they heard Assistant Secretary Doolin's response to charges that American forces had caused this massive flooding: 'The flooding in Viet Nam, as you will recall, generated widespread civilian suffering and that was never the intention nor the result of this pro-gram.'[22] If one accepts Weisberg's premise that interlinkages in ecosystems make the consequences of ecocide necessarily wide-spread, it is difficult to accept such a claim at face value. Much the same could be said of the counterinsurgency strategies of the Guatemalan military, which have included bombing and napalming, burning crops, and poisoning streams to eliminate fishing grounds. The strategy is to force the general population into 'strategic hamlets' in order to separate it from the rebels; but how can such practices avoid inflicting widespread suffering? The same case can be made when military regimes extract resources – trees, topsoil, reefs, and other vital components of ecosystems – in places like Haiti, Burma, and East Timor.[23] In the latter territory, the Indonesian Air Force has reportedly used napalm, chemical warfare, and forest fires to restrict Fretilin movements.[24] In Croatia, the bombing of the Sisak oil refinery and a waste water reservoir released over 100 tonnes of oil and waste into the Sava River.[25] The protracted conflict in Eritrea was another example, as one author suggests: 'The war is now the single most important factor of degradation in Eritrea. The clearing of forest reserves by troops, intense bombing raids of civilian targets, the scattering of land mines over wide areas and the concentration of people in and around security hamlets ... And the constant use of heavy weapons, including MiG aircraft carrying napalm and defoliants; a policy of bush clearance of areas believed to be guerilla hideouts; and the Ethiopian troops' demand for fuelwood have all greatly reduced plant cover.[26]

The present Iraqi regime has provided the most vivid example of environmental destruction, whether this was its intention or not. As Iraqi troops retreated from Kuwait, they deliberately spilled oil into the Persian Gulf, killing over 20,000 sea birds and producing an oil slick 100 km long and 30 km wide. And though the oil well fires set by the Iraqis did not produce the ecocatastrophe predicted by some, local damage has been severe. Agricultural activity around the village of Al-Wafrah (close to Kuwait's southern border) was brought to a sudden stop as the huge smoke plume curtailed photosynthesis, oil droplets coated vegetation, and the village lost its water supply.[27] Kuwait City itself escaped such disastrous effects only because of the seasonal Shamal winds. More recently, by constructing a myriad of canals to interrupt the rivers that once filled the marshes of southern Iraq, Saddam Hussein's forces have compelled thousands of Sh'ite Muslims to flee from their ancestral homeland; in this way the regime has certainly committed ecocide, and probably genocide as well.[28] As mentioned earlier, there is a young tradition within international law to mitigate such activities – especially where they pertain to warfare between states – but it is quite limited in scope and effect. Applying either the ENMOD or the Additional Protocol to the Gulf conflict makes little legal sense, since the main players had not ratified both agreements (Iraq has ratified neither), and it is difficult to argue that they constitute customary law.[29]

Military Preparation

What of the second dimension of our first understanding of ecocide – the often disastrous results of war preparation? This would not qualify under Weisberg's initial definition of the term, since it takes place within nations, not across them, and since it is not deliberate ecological damage but rather is incidental to some higher purpose – in this case the 'national security' of the state.

There can be little doubt that military preparation has many environmental effects. Westing places the major environmental impacts of military operations during peacetime in four broad categories: establishing military fortifications and other facilities, equipping and supplying armed forces with weapons and other needs, training armed forces, and routinely deploying those forces.[30] These activities, all of them legitimized in the interests of *national* security, jeopardize *global* security. Johan Galtung asserts that preparation for military activity damages the cosmosphere, the atmosphere, the lithosphere, the iosphere, and, finally, the homosphere.[31] Even seemingly innocuous operations can inflict this damage. For example, there is growing concern in Canada about the effects of the PCBs (which are particularly hazardous when they reach local food chains) that were left behind by the transformers that were used in the NORAD northern warning system.[32]

There is little doubt that the biggest polluter in the United States is the Pentagon. The military's 'toxic empire' – more than 20,000 sites contaminated with millions of tons of toxins and hazardous chemicals – is the subject of a book by Seth Shulman.[33] Only 404 of the 20,000 sites on U.S. Defense Department land have been cleaned up. The Pentagon produces well over a ton of toxic waste every minute. This rivals the output of the top five American chemical companies combined. Though a great deal of money is being spent to clean them up, former weapons plants like those at Hanford, Washington, Savannah River, South Carolina, and Rocky Flats, Colorado, have with ironic flair been termed 'national sacrifice zones.'[34]

Investigations have discovered plutonium in the soil at Rocky Flats; silos containing waste from uranium processing at the Fernald Feed materials site in Ohio; and buried transuranic waste at a laboratory in Idaho. But the most infamous case is probably that of the Hanford Plant, where leaking and unstable single-shell tanks are stored that contain high-level waste. The Hanford site, which produced the plutonium used for the Nagasaki bomb, sits on 300,000 acres of southeast Washington. Stored there in 177 tanks are high-level liquid and semisolid wastes containing radiation and chemicals. Of the 149 older tanks, 66 have been identified as leakers. An alarming 60 per cent of all U.S. high-level waste is stored at Hanford. There are concerns that the hydrogen gas generated in some of the tanks could explode. Local groundwater has been contaminated, and it enters the Columbia River. On top of all this, it is known that in the 1940s, radioactive iodine 131 was deliberately released from the Hanford plant. The DOE has admitted that these airborne releases were large enough to cause health risks to nearby residents. Even today, waste water containing radioactive materials and hazardous chemicals from cooling systems continues to be dumped into the soil at 33 Hanford locations (the DOE planned to discontinue this practice by June 1995). The cost of cleaning up this mess is estimated at $57 billion, and in May of 1989 Washington officials, DOE, and the Environmental Protection Agency signed an agreement to complete the job by 2019. Meanwhile, a DOE report completed in July 1992 but not released until February 1993 concluded that 'the condition of the tank farms is poor and continues to deteriorate further because corrective maintenance is not keeping up with the equipment failure and the tank farm upgrade program is not being implemented fast enough.'[35]

As daunting a task as it will no doubt prove to be (initial optimism that it could be done in thirty years or less has faded), the Americans will not only be responsible for a domestic clean-up. American installations elsewhere – especially in Europe – accumulated significant waste during the Cold War.[36] The Soviet Union left a similar legacy in Eastern Europe.

It is a rather dismal fact, but the Americans' problems with radioactive waste pale in comparison to those being faced by citizens of the former Soviet Union. Even before the break-up of the old Soviet empire, two Soviet analysts asserted that the largest single contribution to environmental problems in that vast region was military production.[37] State secrecy long hid the true extent of what is now known to be nothing less than a catastrophic situation. As new information comes to light it is becoming clearer and clearer that the Soviet civil and military nuclear programs were planned with shocking negligence and ineptitude. For example, the Russian government has recently disclosed that the giant Mayak plutonium plant, built near Chelyabinsk in 1948, has been the scene of two serious accidents and, worse, that the plant 'dumped radioactive waste into a nearby river during the first seven years of its operation,' thereby affecting more than 450,000 people with radiation.[38] After 1951, wastes from the same Chelyabinsk plant were dumped directly in Lake Karachay, contaminating local groundwater. According to one report, 'the radiation is ... so great today that as little as one hour's exposure at the shoreline could prove fatal.'[39] Parts of the lake had to be covered with concrete because of this wildly irresponsible nuclear-waste dumping.

Given the extent of these environmental problems, we can see why they might be labelled ecocide. However, since problems of this nature are usually interpreted as unfortunate consequences of defence production and systems, and not as intended effects, ecocide will probably retain its original meaning: war against the environment itself. But what is the scope of that war? This is the issue we take up in the next section.

The Second Understanding

In 1971, Clifton Fadiman and Jean White published a book titled *Ecocide ... And Thoughts Toward Survival*. In the introduction, Harvey Wheeler wrote that the 'message of our day is ecocide, the environment being murdered by mankind.' This was typical of much of the early literature of political ecology that emerged in the United States during this period – literature that some might retrospectively label alarmist, others prophetic.[40] Kenneth Watt, who also contributed an article to that book, wrote of the 'ecocidal asymptote,' the stage at which the depletion of a resource mixes with the enhanced technological capacity for its exploitation to produce disaster. War is not the central issue here. The real issue is the broader processes of environmental exploitation; and these are often subsumed into larger processes of historical change, such as imperialism.[41]

In approaching ecocide in this way we cast a rather large net around environmental problems. As mentioned at the beginning of this chapter, Feshbach and Friendly have compiled an excellent book about the Soviet ecological crisis; but their conception of ecocide is rather unclear. They argue that it is the result of 'reckless exploitation, skewed priorities and pernicious neglect.' This is certainly the case. But then they add, 'Ecocide is not just an urban phenomenon. In the Third World it is a burning rainforest or a spreading desert. In the United States its victims include the oystermen of the Chesapeake Bay.'[42] With all due respect to displaced fisheries workers everywhere, one might wonder whether their predicament should be labelled with a term as connotative as ecocide. The volume on the Soviet Union combines ecocide with health concerns: the book covers everything from agricultural policies such as the monoculture of cotton, to rampant alcoholism, political disenchantment, and inadequate medical services. It is a sweeping and careful indictment of the Soviet central planning system, but it is rather liberal with the term that leads its title. A more accurate term might have been *ecocatastrophe*, though this risks confusing human-induced with natural disasters.[43]

This line of argument has great contemporary resonance in the literature that focuses on the connections between social structures and the environmental crises many nations face. Ecofeminism has emerged as a central variant, one that links violence against women with violence against nature on a global level through the 'capitalist patriarchal world system.'[44] Ecocide arises from a technology-based approach to human survival; it has resulted from the modes of production characterizing various human epochs, and/or from the cultural institutions that have given impetus to those modes of production. All of this attempts to describe and/or explain the rise and continuation of environmental problems from a nonscientific perspective (i.e., it goes beyond the technical explanations offered by most ecologists). Ecocide can result not only from war between governments but also from collaboration among them, or between them and certain industries.[45] Interestingly, this conception moves us beyond the notion that the state (through its military apparatus) is the only agent capable of ecocide. Industrial and agricultural sectors, fisheries, vacationers in the tropics, and household product consumers – and ultimately, most of us – become complicit.

Ecocide may thus offer us a label for the process of environmental decay, which has stimulated so many fascinating critical reflections on modern society. However, the term ecocide has limited utility to descriptions of the environmental crisis as a whole. Also, because it signifies so much, it has little to offer us in the way of legal approaches: it is not synonymous with environmental warfare or even with negligence by military and public authorities. Indeed, there is semantic confusion inherent in the term's broader meaning. At first it seems quite appropriate, since the prefix *eco* is from the Greek *oikos*, which translates into *home*. Thus economics is the science of taking care of the home;

ecology is the science of understanding the interactions of parts of the home; and ecocide could be the process of destroying it. It is hard to argue against those who insist that our planet has been experiencing a death of sorts. Though this makes more sense in limited contexts such as torched rainforests, acidified lakes, and toxic waste dumps, the spectre of global warming offers new impetus to the equating of home with globe: as a species, humans may well be destroying their home.

However, *cide* is from the Latin *caedere*, which means 'to kill.' Traditionally, at least, this has implied deliberate murder, as in genocide, infanticide, and even regicide (the killing of kings). While the present author is certainly sympathetic to the argument that in many ways human society has been degrading the environment (and that this process is tied directly to others related to human exploitation), the term *ecocide* connotes intent, such as found in the Americans' actions in Vietnam and the Iraqis' actions in the Persian Gulf. So the maximalist definition goes too far, unless one equates ignorance, confusion, and greed – and even the many acts of resistance and co-operation aimed at stemming the tide of environmental decay – with part of a broader effort to kill off all species but our own.[46]

In terms of institutional responses to this broad understanding of ecocide, there has indeed been a wealth of intergovernmental activity to manage the environment, though critics argue that this activity merely reinforces state power and doesn't go far enough to address the basic causes of environmental degradation. Arrangements are in place to deal with the ozone layer, global warming, marine pollution, transboundary transportation of toxic wastes, whaling, acid rain, and many other threats to environmental security. Whether these arrangements are effective or not is, of course, another issue. While they certainly commit states to action, enforcement is a problem, in that states enter such agreements on voluntary terms. The literature emerging on environmental regimes is generally supportive of their value, but questions remain as to whether these agreements are sufficiently binding to bring about long-term compliance in the face of growing economic competition and globalization. The more trenchant critics complain this 'global managerialist' approach to global environmental problems replicates the centralized decision-making, based on Western technological knowledge, that created the problems in the first place.[47]

There is a sustained body of literature which suggests that the environmental crisis poses such a threat to all life on earth that authoritarian measures are justified – ultimately on a global level – to curtail population growth, resource consumption, pollution, and other ills. This call for a 'green leviathan,' which is conceptually linked to international relations theories espousing hierarchical political organization, has been explored elsewhere.[48] At this point we might add that what is often termed the *ecofascist* approach would be as injurious to human beings as ecocide, assuming that we demand some measure of civil freedom in our conception of human security; and to impose ecological security on the global level would take nothing short of a military crusade, which in itself would have ecocidal tendencies.

Perhaps the maximalist definition of ecocide is simply too broad to be useful. It might be optimal to reserve the term for specific cases of deliberate environmental destruction brought about by tactics and/or strategies of warfare; in this limited sense ecocide would be seen as a device, rather than as a consequence of organized violence or modernity. This limited conception would breathe some life into the legal approaches aimed at mitigating ecocidal events; and although the caveats discussed in the preceding section certainly retain their significance, we might one day see the acceptance of a 'Convention on the Suppression and Punishment of the Crime of Ecocide.' That being said, it would be premature to abandon the maximalist understanding altogether.

If ecocide only takes place during conditions of war, we need an operational definition of *warfare*. And this raises further conceptual difficulties. Surely the destruction of the habitat of indigenous peoples constitutes organized violence against the environment, to those peoples. It is part of a deliberate strategy, interpreted benignly as 'development' by some (though surely not all 'developers' are so naïve). But for those most directly affected it must seem as though war is taking place – as though an attack has been unleashed on their subsistence and human dignity. This too raises tricky questions of definition. Are the low-level flights over Labrador, Canada, by NATO jets a form of ecocide? While it seems obvious to this author (who is aware of the land claims dimension) that such flights disturb wildlife and harm traditional ways of life, the term ecocide, which strongly suggests the irreparable mutilation of ecosystems, seems a rather harsh one in this case. In the end, we are stuck with the usual frustrations that attend any relative term.

Perhaps we are trying too hard to define the wrong word. In the broader sense, and tying this chapter back to our earlier discussion of human and environmental global security, we will always be subject to inherent levels-of-analysis problems. We need to think of personal, collective, and environmental security, each of which provides a human rights agenda. Ecocide is, of course, a fundamental threat to global security – but it is one of many. Here our discussion might benefit from the drawing of some interconnections.

Full Circle?

A growing body of research is connecting violence to environmental degradation. The argument is that ecocide, as maximally defined, leads to conditions of human–human violence, which lead in turn to increased levels of ecocide (in its narrower sense), population displacement, and even genocide. The essential thesis is that the environmental stress caused by excessive human demands on ecosystems can create and/or exacerbate absolute poverty to the point where violence is almost inescapable. One related project focuses on three issues that may lead to violence in Southern nations: water scarcity and degradation, population displacement, and general economic decline.[49] All of this work is empirically rich, and exceeds the conventional limits of security studies, though it does not attempt to define ecocide for us.

Another example of such literature is the Panos Institute's *Greenwar: Environment and Conflict*, which focuses specifically on problems in Africa's Sahel region. The main cause of violence in many parts of that region is the conflict between pastoralists and farmers, two groups whose ways of life were once symbiotic. Unfortunately, with the advent of colonialism these groups have developed into antagonists, and they continue to be so in the postcolonial era.[50] The enclosing of nomads within the confines of modern nation-states led to unsustainable agricultural practices and inevitable conflicts over land use. (This was at the very least a contributory factor in the civil war now raging in Somalia.)[51] The book also covers conflict over three rivers: the Beli (which runs from Mali through Burkina Faso and into Niger), the Senegal, and the Nile. Unfortunately, water conflict studies are proving to be a growth field. The Middle East, which faces increasing water deficits, is the most visible region for such studies, but the problems associated with water conflict there can be found on every continent. It is certainly possible that co-operative arrangements are at least as likely as conflicts, and there are several prominent African examples of such co-operation, including the Unduga Group (Nile basin), the Lake Chad Basin Commission, and the Niger Basin Authority.[52] Indeed, some analysts stress that the problems associated with water have the potential to foster international co-operation, since neighbouring states are obliged to invest in mutually vulnerable infrastructures.[53] This may be an optimistic appraisal. A study by the Center for Strategic and International Studies in Washington listed ten possible water wars, half of them in the Middle East, where there is lingering conflict over access to all three major river systems (the Euphrates, the Jordan, and the Nile).[54] Joyce Starr, arguing that American policymakers have been slow to realize the security implications of water as compared to those of oil, believes that 'water security will soon rank with military security in the war rooms of defense ministries.'[55]

This field of literature will grow more important in the future. The sharing of resources can create co-operative channels of human interaction, but it is obvious that conflict is as readily provoked. The important thing, as our metaphor of a circle suggests, is to avoid falling into an analytic trap of 'environmental determinism.' Environmental stress is certainly important as a variable, but there will always be many other political, social, and economic factors driving people to commit violence. Rwanda is an example: That country has one of the highest population densities in human history, and surely that overcrowding has contributed to the recent mayhem in the country. But many other (perhaps related) factors are also in play, such as Tutsi-Hutu conflict, government oppression, economic depression, pressures from neighbouring states, and so on. The complexity of the problem is, unfortunately, indicative of how difficult it will be to find a workable solution. It should be no surprise to those concerned about national and international security that we can find links between poverty, ecocide, and even genocide; and that the Rwandan case had elements of all.[56]

There is another sense in which our two understandings of ecocide might be seen as complementary or dialectical rather than dichotomous. We shouldn't forget that our second understanding of ecocide – that it is a project of modernity – highlights the importance of the spread of the ideas that make such a process possible. The message of modernity includes the need to *overcome* nature; and as a result of efforts to do so, we have engaged in environmental degradation. In this transmission of ideas, there have been few fertilizers as adept as military preparation and war. The highly televised Gulf War of 1990–91, which was arguably the greatest weapons convention ever held, demonstrated this well. The military's role in the environmental modification of Brazil's Amazon is well known. With regard to changes brought to the Inuit by the militarization of the North, Kevon McMahon believes that 'the military did its most sweeping and profound environmental damage in the Arctic by carpet bombing the place with its political, economic and cultural ideas. As amorphous and insidious as radiation poisoning, they are, finally, much more toxic.'[57]

Conclusion

The final understanding of ecocide that emerges, then, is one of connections: between strategies of war, militarism, broader societal processes, and (without offering apologies for any anthropocentrism this reveals) human rights issues. This chapter concludes that the term ecocide is best employed in its minimalist conception, to describe deliberate acts of environmental carnage by states in a military context. But it might also be used to describe the effects of military preparation or – in a much larger leap of conceptual space – the recent history of human–environment relations on a local and even global scale. All of these understandings lead to a similar conclusion: people must have a fundamental human right to environmental security. Furthermore, the advent of acute ecocide, just like the advent of acute genocide or mass murder, ultimately will result in sudden population movements and the creation of refugees.

However, despite various attempts through international law, environmental security is almost impossible to ensure in the event of armed conflict.[58] This is the case in traditional wars between sovereign states, and in wars against indigenous peoples, and in civil wars within states undergoing fragmentation. At this point we must return to two concepts that were raised in the first chapter: sovereignty and justice. While it is clear that global environmental regimes, weakly defined, are emerging in a number of issue areas, states jealously guard their sovereign right to determine their own natural resource policies.[59] As for justice, we might argue, with Paul Wapner, that environmental problems have disproportionate effects on the people that suffer their consequences. Temporal equality suggests that we must refrain from ecocide now (in any of the understandings discussed above) for the sake of future generations. This is often a hard sell, however, when it comes to actual policy implementation, although the *precautionary principle* (which suggests that we err on the side of caution before embarking on large-scale projects about which we are ultimately uncertain) seems to be making at least rhetorical gains in international environmental diplomacy.[60] Spatial equality suggests that governments should attempt to enact policies and legislation designed to at least minimize this differentiation in effect. The workers displaced by the Canadian cod moratorium, for example, need government assistance, be it to retrain them for other work or to support them temporarily (or, more pessimistically, for a very long time). Wapner uses the concept of environmental displacement, which is 'about exploiting one's shadow ecology. It involves discounting the lives of those who live in areas that supply natural resources or find themselves on the receiving end of the industrial wastestream.'[61] A strong conception of human and global security will keep this concept firmly in mind.

Ecocide, no matter how it is defined, leaves long-lasting scars, not only on the land and sea but also in the psyche of people. It is ultimately a human problem, and one that gives rise to others, such as the refugee crisis that will be discussed in the next chapter. As I.G. Simmons writes with regard to one of the indelible physical impressions of local ecology resulting from the First World War, 'the cemeteries are a permanent land use change.'[62] This might be the starkest symbol of the full circle which, with appropriate trepidation, we have drawn around our two understandings of ecocide.

And if the second understanding seems more appropriate today, then we might keep this mind during our later discussion of the nascent term globalization. The implications are disturbing, since we seem bent on a course that has derived its speed from our ability to rapidly exploit the environment in the name of a vision of progress defined chiefly by Western industrial forces.

4

Population Displacement: Refugees[1]

refugee: *n.* person taking refuge, esp. in foreign country from war or persecution or natural disaster. [F *refugie* (prec.)]

The Oxford Dictionary of Current English (1986), 626

This chapter opens with a stubborn normative statement: Human security is a moot concept if it doesn't apply to everyone, including those who have fallen outside the realm of traditionally recognized political collectivities.

The previous two chapters explored concepts that describe human suffering and, as often, movement. War, genocide, starvation, ecocide, environmental degradation: all of these elements conspire to force millions of people to leave their homelands each year and the international community, despite the intense efforts of the UN (a financially constrained and largely reactive body) and several nongovernmental organizations, finds it a struggle to deal with this phenomenon. In this age of genocide, ecocide, and globalization, who are refugees? And how do they fit into conceptions of global human and environmental security? Who are the *truly* homeless – those without community membership, those on the run from forces beyond their control? And what institutional response (if any) is in order that requires reconceptualizing?

As usual, there is a minimalist understanding of the term refugee, one which corresponds to an international Convention that defines the term and provides an official mandate to that over-worked international organization mentioned earlier, the United Nations High Commissioner for Refugees (UNHCR). Refugee, in this context, amounts to a political term; and regardless of rising population levels, economic and political instability, gender discrimination, and whatever other events and processes are taking place in the age of globalization, this old, narrow definition continues to dominate in the policymaking and academic contexts. But there is also a maximalist conception with which we may contrast the more conventional definition, and it relates to what some have called economic or, in even more popular parlance, *environmental refugees*.

The latter phrase has gained considerable currency in recent years. Most contemporary texts dealing with global environmental problems make dutiful mention of the coming refugee crisis and its clear links to environmental degradation and, especially, climate change.[2] Should the sea level rise, as is commonly predicted, millions of citizens in Bangladesh, Egypt, China, India, and various ocean islands will be in need of new homes.[3] It is also believed that Africa will be disproportionately affected by the contributions to global climate change made by other, more industrialized regions; this will lead to increased population movements as the search for sustenance moves people within nations and across borders.[4] Moreover, the long-term effects of poverty in the south will encourage still more people to leave their communities in search of employment and personal security.

Yet there is no need to rely solely on future projections. The plight of those already displaced – by soil erosion in sub-Saharan Africa, by dam construction in South America and Asia, by deforestation in the Himalayas, and by war in any number of regions – makes it quite obvious that we must consider these internal and external migrants victims of political problems that lack immediate solutions. This phenomenon is not limited to the South: the flood of Russians and Ukrainians from the Chernobyl area after the 1986 nuclear reactor accident, and predictions of an exodus from the depleted East Coast fisheries region in

Canada, make this clear. That being said, the problem of cross-border migration will remain greatest where populations are largest and, arguably, where political regimes are least stable: the South. We must agree with Volker Turk that 'the refugee problem is, more than ever before, a Third World problem, the response of which is an expression of the conflict between the north and the south.'[5]

This chapter will examine the contemporary meaning of the term *refugee* and comment on its appropriateness with regard to the activities of the UNHCR, the body with the most explicit mandate to deal with refugee problems. First, however, we will discuss briefly a model of the contemporary refugee problem that was introduced by Harto Hakovirta in 1993. In keeping with the preceding chapters, we will sharply distinguish the minimalist and maximalist positions before discussing their institutional implications.

A quick caveat: The UNHCR (along with many other organizations, both official and nonstate) is involved in confronting the important question of the *environmental impact* of refugees. But this is quite different from confronting the various contributory *environmental causes* of refugees. We will make it clear that even if redefining certain migrants as environmental refugees were politically feasible – which it currently is not – the UNHCR alone is in no position to carry out such a vastly extended mandate. This is all the more true if we include the internally displaced, as many analysts now suggest we should. Unfortunately, this strengthens arguments against humanitarian interventions (and, it follows, for the absolute paramountcy of state sovereignty regardless of the situation 'on the ground'). In this chapter we will argue that contemporary, non-Convention refugees must be viewed within the context of two overlapping phenomena: the global refugee and migration crisis (brought on by warfare and economic dislocation), and the global environmental crisis (brought on by factors discussed in the previous chapter). Separating refugees into groups for analytic convenience is not necessarily going to contribute to an improvement in their lot. The same logic applies to those fleeing from destitute poverty: although their plight is often related to violence, they fall outside the parameters of the legal, minimalist definition; yet expanding that definition to include them does not necessarily help their situation.

From a global perspective, the problem may well be too large for international organizations to handle, and bilateral initiatives will be needed alongside open immigration policies and long-term aid. However, this seems less likely as governments in the North confront their own financial realities, which are doing much to shape their external aid budgets. As well, xenophobia continues to be a factor in immigration policy, and fears of Third World population increases provoke it. This, at a time when *enlightened self-interest* is as important a concept as ever. The South's current condition is at least partly the result of exploitation by the North, yet the North is finding itself less and less able to contribute to long-term solutions. The South could well be left largely to its own devices to deal with the coming environmental refugee crisis. It is fairly safe to predict that the North will offer only minimal assistance.[6] This chapter will conclude, then, with a discussion of this age of troubled humanitarianism, and of the need to avoid parochialism in the nation-state system.

Though doing so would have certain merits, creating a new, 'maximalist' category of refugees would not in itself solve anything. This is because there are no international means at present to deal with such a new, overarching category in a sustained manner, and because it is the *roots* of environmentally and economically induced migration that need pulling – and this would involve much more energy, intuition, and commitment than the international community has so far demonstrated. Finally, to apply the maximalist definition of the term would be to include the internally displaced. This, of course, would set aside the essential state-centricity of the minimalist definition, and cause legal confusion in the process. While most displacement occurs within, rather than across borders – even in situations of acute violence – the UNHCR at present is unable in most cases to deal with this phenomenon because it has no mandate to do so. Giving it one would mean entrusting an international organization with the right to override the principle of nonintervention, and this, as our discussion of genocide suggested, is a rather difficult proposition, despite recent NATO intervention in Serbia.

I would add a brief note concerning the most extended maximalist position on this term. Some have suggested that in an age of globalization, during which borders are becoming meaningless, and during which space and time have compressed as a result of technological advances, we are all refugees of a sort. In other words, states don't really matter any longer: we live in a vacuum, and without political loyalties, and correspondingly we suffer from some of the same disorientation and lack of direction as many refugees. While there are intriguing possibilities here, I will refrain from incorporating this ultra-maximalist position into this chapter. To do so would be extremely premature, and might even mock the condition of real refugees. Only in the refugee issue-area does it become so apparent that borders *do* matter, both to states protecting them and to those trying to cross them. Here we will put aside our postmodern angst, and move to a discussion of a less abstract maximalist conception of our term.

Economic/Environmental Refugees

The literature on refugees tends to lump those who cross borders together with those who do not. This presents obvious problems for existing international law, which is still (to the frustration of many critics) based on a state-centric world. The main question at hand here relates to the connection between displacement and economic dislocation. The latter refers to changed circumstances that make survival exceptionally difficult, such as the economic chaos in Haiti and the immediate effects of relaxing price controls and instituting privatization in the former Soviet Union. Environmental refugees would also include those forced to move due to planetary warming, increased ultraviolet radiation, loss of productive soil, loss of fisheries resources, natural hazards such as volcanoes and hurricanes, and industrial hazards such as toxic waste dumping and lethal accidents. The analytic focus so far has been on the factors that force people to leave their homes; less attention has been paid to where they will go.

The most commonly accepted definition of *environmental refugee* is the one offered by El-Hinnawi for the United Nations Environmental Program in 1985: an environmental refugee is 'a person who has been forced to leave their traditional habitat, temporarily or permanently because of a marked environmental disruption (natural and/or triggered by humans) that jeopardized their existence and/or seriously affected the quality of their life.'[7] In the mid-1980s, with the support of the Federal Republic of Germany, the UN General Assembly established a Group of Environmental Experts on International Co-operation to Avert New Flows of Refugees. This group produced an inconclusive report that categorized the causes of refugee movements as either natural or man-made (political and socioeconomic); it also argued that violations of human rights and fundamental freedoms were contributors to the latter.[8] This is indeed the case. In Burma, the heavily criticized SLORC regime took advantage of roads built by Thai timber firms following a bilateral logging agreement signed in 1989, to defeat minority rebel groups whose hide-outs had until then been unapproachable.[9] It was ecological destruction that afforded SLORC this military opportunity. Such linkages, rather too subtle for international law, leave room for manoeuvering, given the precedent of the Cartagena Declaration. In other words, we may already have in place the mandate to help environmental refugees. But we must also be aware of the complexity and enormity of the refugee issue today.

It is extremely difficult to estimate the number of refugees worldwide, especially if one seeks to include internally displaced persons. Arthur Westing has estimated that in 1990 there were almost 17 million recognized cross-border refugees and 3.5 million unrecognized; while there may have been over 21 million unrecognized 'internal refugees.'[10] Jon Martin Trolldalen has estimated that there are some 10 million environmental refugees today, half of whom are in sub-Saharan Africa.[11] When

G.J. van Hof euren Goedhart was appointed the first High Commissioner for Refugees in 1951, there were 1,250,000 recognized refugees. In 1976, with Sadruddin Aga Khan as High Commissioner, there were still only 2.8 million. In 1994, by contrast, there were over 19 million, and this figure was taken before the recent frenzy of violence in (and resultant exodus from) Rwanda in April–May 1994.[12] This movement has occurred in the context of greatly expanded population movements in general: in 1989 the UN estimated that some 50 million people, or one per cent of the world's population, lived in countries other than their country of origin, and the World Bank estimated international migrants of all kinds at 100 million.[13] Scenarios of global climate change predict that there will be much more migration as larger and larger areas become virtually uninhabitable.[14] The resulting economic disparity will only add to the tendency of people to physically remove themselves from impoverished areas in search of land, food, warmth, and security.

Alongside this unprecedented increase in numbers there has evolved a much more complex understanding of refugee and migration issues. While political refugees were once regarded as 'the tragic product of an incompatible juxtaposition, whether of faction, class, religion, ideology, or nationality,' other factors such as development, overpopulation, and the environment play a major role today, necessitating even more complex models.[15] Much of the traditional literature on population movements takes as its explanatory base what Kavanagh and Lonergan term the *neo-classical economics' equilibrium approach*, which stresses individuals making optimal and largely economically oriented decisions; but a growing body of research now stresses, instead, macrostructural factors such as social inequity, both within and across borders.[16] This moves us quite logically toward a maximalist definition of the term refugee. Coincident with this approach is work that focuses on the environmental origins of conflict, such as land use patterns and water scarcity leading to violence and population displacement (a concept introduced in the previous chapter on ecocide).[17] For example, the most serious environmental threats produced by the prolonged civil war in Mozambique are the result of displaced citizens converging suddenly on safety zones along the coast and near the Zimbabwe border.[18] Refugees are usually the product of political and/or economic variables, and often the direct result of war-induced displacement. An influx of 100,000 refugees into rural sub-Saharan Africa may desertify some 875 acres of once arable land, and create annual demands for more than 100,000 tons of firewood.[19] Such empirical factors call for models of refugee crises more advanced than the traditional 'push-pull' versions.

One of the more inclusive models has been offered by Harto Hakovirta of the Department of Government and International Relations at the University of Lapland, Finland. Hakovirta views the global refugee problem as having seven interconnected factor clusters. The first five are conflict situations, the organization and activities of refugees themselves (an important element, often overlooked), the character of specific refugee situations, development (suggesting the importance of economic factors such as employment and long-term financial security), and the environment. To these five, Hakovirta adds two more. The first is the internationalization of refugee situations, 'the processes through which refugee situations evoke international attention, become objects of international debates, and move upwards on the international agenda.' The term refugee is contestable precisely because of this phenomenon, as evidence by the widespread coverage of population movements in the former Yugoslavia and Rwanda (see Chapter 2). The second is the managing and resolving of refugee situations: 'efforts by organizations and states, as motivated by humanitarian concerns and interest calculations, to protect and otherwise assist refugees, to help affected countries, and to ease the situation as a whole.'[20] The divisions are logical and, given the inherent complexity of the issue, help order a broad analytic undertaking. Socioeconomic factors are no longer relegated to the obscure or incidental.

But this is an *academic* definition, and policymakers must ultimately apply an *operative* definition of the term refugee when determining who should receive the commensurate status. If someone is suffering from political persecution – is at danger of becoming a victim of genocide, or state-sponsored torture, for example – then this seems a clear case. However – and this pushes us slightly toward a maximalist position – we might ask about practices that are condemned in some quarters but accepted in others. In the process of fostering human security, we must find ways to deal with the relativist/universalist split in understandings of human rights. Some argue that *any* severe threat to human security – including discrimination, environmental decay, and economic upheaval – should be folded into definitions of refugee status. This would be a maximalist position, of course, though it is not entirely rejected in the actual legal world, since individual states set their own refugee/immigration policies, and do not necessarily adhere to the Convention.

Example: One of the more complex refugee issues involves those fleeing from female genital mutilation (often called female circumcision). This is the practice, found in some Islamic areas, of removing or altering parts of the female genitalia at a certain age as a rite of passage. Generally, one of two procedures is involved: *infibulation*, the severing of the clitoris and labia while the two sides of the vulva are sutured (tied together); or *clitoridectomy*, the partial or complete removal of the clitoris or the removal of both the clitoris and the labia minora.

Both procedures have come under severe criticism from many quarters, yet they are also defended as a cultural priority in others. When a newspaper in Liberia published a series of articles critical of the custom, it became the target of a hostile protest movement by a group of local women. Several Western states, including Canada and the United States, have made it illegal for doctors to perform the procedure. This is quite significant, as large numbers of recently arrived African women live in both states. There is no strong opposition to the practice at the international level, though UN agencies such as the World Health Organization generally oppose it on health grounds.

Female genital mutilation can result in excessive bleeding, infection, and even death when improperly performed, and its after-effects include the risk of childbirth complications and possible development of obstetric fistulae – holes between the vagina and the bladder and/or rectum. Many women view the practice as an act of oppression because it denies women a form of sexual pleasure.[21] Thus the issue has become a rallying cry for the feminist movement in general, above and beyond other Islamic customs, such as purdah, which have come under intense criticism by Western feminists. The international implications of this condemnation can be seen in Canadian refugee policy, which recently began to include women fleeing persecution on the basis of discrimination against their sex as valid candidates for asylum. However, most women who undergo the procedure are too young to leave their native countries on their own, or lack the resources to do so.

This is a gender-related issue that compels us to ask whether the definition of a refugee should conform with strict political parameters or should include those fleeing from societal practices they perceive as threatening to their life, liberty, or happiness. Governments will have to seriously consider this matter when directing development assistance toward health programs abroad, and when determining their own operational definitions of refugee status.

All of this aside, many refugee situations will continue to involve large-scale movements induced by war, environmental degradation, and/or severe economic dislocation. How will the primary international institution devoted to this issue-area deal with calls for a maximalist position?

Institutional Implications: The UNHCR

The UNHCR should be seen as part of three interlinked constellations of international organizations. First, it is partly the product of a normative element, international humanitarianism. The origins of contemporary refugee relief efforts date back to the 1800s with the establishment of the League of the Red Cross and

Red Crescent and the extraordinary work of Fridtjof Nansen (1861–1930). There have since been many other international efforts and instruments established to protect and relieve the victims of warfare. One can be cynical about humanitarianism, but it is difficult to deny its beneficial effects altogether.

Second, the UNHCR exists as unit of the United Nations system itself.[22] The system has attracted adherents to a multilateral regime that has evolved to mitigate the harm suffered by refugees, though many countries that have joined the regime have done so with reservations.[23] The UN system has, of course, become the overarching framework for intergovernmental organization; it dominates most discussions on the future of internationalism and on the implementation of the humanitarian impulse that drives efforts such as refugee assistance. Yet as any cursory observer would note, the UN is in a state of perpetual flux; it cannot take initiatives without the approval of member states, and its form and function are challenged by both current events such as the war in Serbia and by internal and external suggestions for major changes. The UNHCR will always be subject to the vagaries of the institutional complexity of the UN itself.

Third, the UNHCR operates within the confines of the global political system. One hesitates to add this obvious yet deeply complicating feature, since there are as many understandings of the international system as there are aspiring understanders. Sovereignty remains the dominant feature of the formal global political system; 'globalization' along neoliberal lines is the dominant force in the informal economic sphere. The former precludes the existence of a central authority that might give organizations like the UNHCR the clout to enforce a mandate (the frustrating treatment of the UNHCR in Bosnia provides a good illustration). The latter reinforces the drive for industrialization, and increases the likelihood of a greater refugee problem in the future. In this complicated world, international organizations operate with little autonomy. Yet despite the Soviet Union's absence of support during the Cold War, the UNHCR has been able to retain what in retrospect has been a remarkable image as an autonomous agency, free from the usual complaints that UN agencies are the foreign policy instruments of the great powers or pawns in a larger East–West or, increasingly, North–South, struggle for world domination. (As we shall see, this may be changing.)

The UNHCR is an extension of earlier refugee assistance programs, which were developed initially for post–World War adjustments and for specific incidents such as the exodus of Russians from the Bolshevik Revolution. The UN Convention Relating to the Status of Refugees, and with it the UNHCR, was not formally established until 1951. Though it was intended as an apolitical mission – and to some extent considered as one – the Soviet Union did not support it. Thus it was identified with Western interests throughout the Cold War. (The United States had legislation until 1980 that defined refugees as people fleeing communism.) The UNHCR was instrumental both in transborder resettlement emergencies and in repatriation projects. The most recent of the latter, largely viewed as a success, was the repatriation of some 300,000 Cambodians from Thailand in the summer of 1993. But the question of environmental and poverty-linked problems has remained quite peripheral to the organization until recently.

In 1992 the General Assembly welcomed 'the proposal of the High Commissioner to appoint an environmental coordinator responsible for developing guidelines and taking other measures for incorporating environmental considerations into the programs of the Office of the HC ... in view of the impact on the environment of the large numbers of refugees and displaced persons.'[24]

A close reading of the above makes it clear that this official, the Coordinator on Environmental Affairs, is charged with examining and orienting policy toward not the environmental *causes* of refugees, but rather the environmental *impacts* of refugees.[25] This is undeniably important (and understaffed) work: any large-scale refugee settlement will create unprecedented strains on local ecology. But it does not get at the question of refugee movements *caused*, at least in part, by environmental problems, nor for that matter does it point to the socioeconomic patterns that give rise to mass population movements.

At present the UNHCR is in no position to deal with such a large question. Rather, it seems more practical to focus on integrating the work of relief and development agencies, with preventive action – or at least the best actions possible given the constraints of the international system – as a goal. This gives rise to calls for a 'cross-mandate approach,' though again we are likely to see more reactive than preventive efforts. An example of these is the World Bank's involvement in a reforestation program in Pakistan, which was designed to repair the damage caused by the influx of over two million Afghan refugees to the Northwest Frontier Province and Baluchistan. The list of intergovernmental organizations involved in refugee assistance is a long one; it includes the International Organization for Migration, UNICEF, the World Food Program, the World Health Organization, and the UN Disaster Relief Organization. As well, the Department of Humanitarian Affairs has a mandate to act 'as the focal point for the UN system for an early warning mechanism for emergencies, which will have to include environmental refugees.'[26] Also, many nongovernmental organizations (NGOs), such as the Red Cross, are involved on the ground in the refugee crisis. This leads some analysts, such as Donald Puchala, to believe that the increasingly important role of NGOs must be recognized and 'more formally built into the system.'[27] Indeed, refugee relief and prevention is an excellent area for the study of the interactions between intergovernmental and transnational actors. We must also keep in mind that some nongovernmental actors are in fact political actors with military agendas. For example, in the huge refugee camps in Zaire that sprang up following the Rwandan genocide of 1994, the Hutu militias have quite clearly taken control, and are even training new recruits on camp grounds. 'Those refugees who have expressed the desire to go back have been threatened or killed by the militias. The militias also instill … fear that they will be killed by the RPF [Rwandan Patriotic Front] upon their return … The UNHCR and other aid groups have been forced to accept the authority of the militias.'[28] But what of the original question raised: the conceptual dimension to changing the mandate of the UNHCR to include *socioeconomic* or *environmental refugees*? Does it make sense to move toward the maximalist definition?

At first glance, it seems simple enough: these people are fleeing their homelands, and in doing so entering either other counties or other parts of their own county. They have no choice in the matter, if they wish to suvive, and thus they should be granted refugee status, even if that means the official mandate of the UNHCR must be permanently expanded. Yet many disagree, feeling that the UNHCR lacks the resources to cope with such an expanded mandate (in simple financial terms, this is certainly true at present). The director of the U.S. Committee for Refugees believes that we are in fact discussing a possible increase in the number of 'economic/environmental migrants.' He admits this is probably 'too simple a term but is better than using the word "refugee" [which] would be harmful to the protection and assistance efforts of those working for people fleeing *persecution*.'[29] This is a good point. If refugee status automatically implies the right to asylum (which it usually does), then it will be extremely difficult to get governments to accept the proposition. The American response to the Haitian escapees makes it clear that even the largest industrialized nations lack the will to comply with asylum rights.[30] Pushing millions more refugees onto the agenda could weaken this resolve even further. Our earlier discussion of genocide suggested that there will be a need for persecution-related refugee asylum in the future.

The director of the UN's Department of Humanitarian Affairs believes that a 'wrong message would be sent to people if UNHCR's mandate, the uniqueness of which derives from the protection clause, was to include economic or environmental causes of internal displacement or external movement.'[31] A veteran of the UNHCR itself had a similar response, stressing the immense task with which the office is already charged: 'I worked for the UNHCR for ten years. Its mandate is already overstretched to include persons internally displaced due to violence and warfare, when the UN Secretary General so requests.'[32]

There is little doubt that the UNHCR is in a perpetual financial crisis, despite the heroic fundraising efforts of its current High Commissioner, Sadako Ogata. Its 1994 budget was little more than one billion dollars, one-third of which was spent on repatriation. Despite its contemporary importance, it is one of the least institutionalized units in the UN system: as Rosemary Rogers points out, 'the organization is alive and well, but, paradoxically, its mandate is still temporary, having to be renewed at five-year intervals.'[33] This leads to suggestions to change the mechanics of funding – for example, from a voluntary system to 'one based on regular and independent allocation of funds to the Commission.'[34] The editor-in-chief of the *International Journal of Refugee Law* agrees, asserting the 'UNHCR needs a regular budget, not one subject to voluntary contributions and the whims of national interest.'[35] While this is certainly true, such a development is unlikely, given the current financial situation; and we are still left with the question of mandate.

Many, the present author included, are cautious on conceptual grounds. When we label a group of refugees 'economic' or 'environmental,' we simplify their circumstances, invoking images of natural disaster and thereby masking the human causes of their plight: short-sighted government policies, international and civil warfare, the actions of large corporations, and the global warming that is a consequence of a ferocious dependence on industrialization. Jo Ann McGregor feels that the 'addition of the prefix "environmental" to the category "refugee" is unhelpful for a number of reasons ... There is the misleading implication that environmental change as a cause of flight can be meaningfully separated from political and economic changes.'[36] She is less concerned about simplifying the refugees' plight than she is about the environmental problems that gave rise to it.

It is obvious that the 'problem' of human displacement due to environmental degradation and economic dislocation will increase in scope and depth; there will be more and more refugees and their circumstances will become even more precarious as the likelihood of their going home (or, to adopt refugee parlance, repatriation) diminishes.

In terms of relief operations for refugees in general, there is a trend toward what many concerned with human security would consider an enlightened approach. David Keen's recent book is a welcome addition to the literature on relief programs. He emphasizes that refugees are not the charity cases that Western nations in particular so often assume them to be. In fact, the paternalism that characterizes their treatment only worsens their plight. A reorientation toward empowering refugees is called for: refugees must be allowed to make decisions, women refugees must be given a greater role, and refugees' diverse economic strategies should be encouraged, not stunted by centralized bureaucracies and relocation programs.

In terms of current and anticipated relief efforts, it is vital that the UNHCR and the World Food Program receive adequate funding; it is also painfully obvious, as Sadako Ogata complains, that these groups aren't receiving it. In a brief Foucaldian analysis, Keen asks this question: Can a system in which refugee camps actually serve the interests of host governments be expected to provide the normative or financial context for needed expansion? And he opens the greatest Pandora's Box of all when he proposes that 'a UN agency should be given a mandate to address the needs of internal refugees, also known as the internally displaced. The agency should have a guaranteed right of access to those in need of relief.'[37] The difficulty here is with the word 'guaranteed.' At present, the UNHCR can carry out internal work only if 'invited.' Interestingly, the term 'displaced persons' did appear in the constitution of the earlier International Refugee Organization, but was dropped from the statute of the UNHCR. Several UN resolutions have authorized the UNHCR to protect and assist people who have left their country of origin for reasons of displacement, as opposed to direct political persecution. However, this does not mean that it has any right of access vis-à-vis internal operations. While the harsh reality of starving millions in southern Sudan is very disturbing, no international coalition has expressed a serious interest in moving in forcefully to stop it. Such measures raise obvious issues about sovereignty, interventionism, financing, and decision making.

Many would like to see the UN adopt a greater role in emergency relief, though how one defines an emergency is highly contestable. What about indigenous people displaced by development-oriented environmental alteration? Many of them would probably reject paternalistic aid. And besides, who would pay for this expansion? Keen's book is less concerned about the incentives and constraints facing donors than about the assertion that refugees have a fundamental right to relief that is enshrined in international law. This is an entirely different assertion, however, when the discusion centres on the internally displaced, who may well number in the hundreds of millions. And still more questions arise when we consider the implications of intervening to stop potential flows of economic refugees. There have been isolated attempts to reorder political society (as seen, for example, in Haiti in the mid to late 1990s); but generally, large donor states will continue to be reluctant to actually change socioeconomic conditions.[38] Such intrusion is only justified, it seems, when the International Monetary Fund decides it is necessary in order to maintain balances of payments for the sake of the broader world economy.

Another, much more immediate factor should be stressed. Those engaged in relief efforts and peacemaking are emerging from the playing field of world politics with a good deal more dirt on their uniforms than ever before. In the context of peacekeeping operations, this is quite obvious, and it is a theme that emerged in our discussion of genocide as well. It is now highly risky in political terms to send troops into peacekeeping operations, as the bloodshed in Bosnia, Cambodia, and Somalia has demonstrated. Relief agencies like the UNHCR can hardly avoid facing similarly dangerous circumstances, whether or not they receive adequate protection from military forces. And there is the further issue of longevity in relief operations, a problem familiar to students of international organization. As one UN official, who wished to remain anonymous, noted to the present author: 'Often the emergency situation can muster much compassion and assistance, but once the acuteness has diminished, interest in providing continued support toward self-reliance dissipates, leaving a chronic or latent emergency situation.'

The UNHCR is but one of many organizations that will be called upon to micromanage the world's increasing array of disaster areas. On its own, it is hardly capable of offering a future quick fix to what many fear will be a tremendous source of conflict – what we may, in an effort to refine a complex topic, term *ecopolitical displacement*. This term has many advantages: it clearly acknowledges ecological factors; it does not complicate the refugee/persecution issue; it brings the internally displaced 'into the fold'; it highlights the anthropogenic dimension of most refugee situations; and through the word 'displacement,' it emphasizes the basic human right to environmental security.

An Age of Troubled Humanitarianism

Environmental and economic refugees are unfortunate victims of forces unique to this century, and they must be viewed from the perspective of global population movements, and of the increases in conflict and ecological stress that those movements cause. What, then, is the outlook for the problem?

There is an understandable fear that whatever humanitarian ethic exists in world politics today is 'fading as the siege mentality/garrison state perspective gains ground.'[39] There is indeed an old lineage of linking refugee problems to immigration polices to political circumstances to economic conditions. The author of an exhaustive report on the pre–Second World War refugee situation concluded that the refugee crisis was

> a world problem in the sense that the existence of refugees is a symptom of the disappearance of economic and political liberalism. Refugees are the by-products of an economic isolationism which has practically stopped free migration; they are the products of the population pressures in Europe which result in part from the paralysis of international trade and the restriction of markets; they symbolize in a most tragic way the development of political

authoritarianism. The basic real solution of the refugee problem, real or potential, is necessarily therefore related to the solution of the great problems of economic and political adjustment in the contemporary world.[40]

Unfortunately, the development of 'globalization' and economic interdependence in later decades (discussed at length in the next chapter) has hardly curtailed the refugee problem and, many would argue, has in fact exacerbated it by increasing overall environmental degradation and economic dislocation while presenting people with greater opportunities for travelling long distances. The last sentence quoted, therefore, remains highly salient. Yet the recognition that there is a global crisis may not always result in the paroxysm of collective identity that some would hope for. It may even breed parochialism, an aggressive denial of the world's interdependence.

Countering this are arguments that we *can* move toward a collective perspective, and that human rights and environmental security should be foreign policy pillars instead of simply sources of reactive impulses.[41] Mel Gurtov's global humanism prescribes four basic solutions to the global refugee crisis: (1) Resources must go to asylum countries for self-sustenance. (2) Indigenous populations in the host area should receive aid. (3) Assistance must go to the countries from which refugees come to alleviate the pressures initially causing them to move, and also to stimulate the prospect of repatriation. (4) The North must embark on a policy of progressive debt relief for the South.[42] As well, of course, the North must open its borders as wide as possible – a contentious issue at the best of times, and one on which intelligent public debate is essential.

Central to prescriptions such as Gurtov's are calls for greater North–South co-operation in an attempt to alleviate what can only be described as a mutual predicament. Without such a normative context, the efforts of relief organizations seem not only futile but conservative. For example, in relation to immigration polices, a strengthened UNHCR can be of only limited long-term advantage if borders are effectively closed. What seems to be at stake is the apolitical nature of the UNHCR, which in an increasingly bifurcated world appears more and more (as an article in *The New York Times* quoted in an earlier footnote suggests) to be a protector of Western borders shrouded in a cloak of humanitarianism. Anthony Richmond is even blunter: 'The most economically developed and affluent countries are banding together to protect their privileged position in much the same way that Afrikaners and others of European descent sought to maintain their dominance in South Africa.'[43] Notions that the UNHCR is a *functionalist* organization, established with relative autonomy to handle problems the nation-state no longer can, are being subsumed by a structuralist perspective that views international organizations as parts of the problem, not potential solutions.[44] To be even more dramatic: We are constantly on the precipice of global barbarism, of a closed and parochial world in which the power relations that now characterize northern dominance are at last stripped of the vestiges of legitimacy, and in which an irrational spiral of insecurity suffocates humanitarian aspirations.

One might argue that environmentally induced population movements are beginning to stress the world economy; and that the humanitarian ethos will eventually be replaced – and for the good – with an ethos of sustainable development. While this is certainly logical (and allowing that political persecution will remain very important in the refugee context), it is by no means clear that it will actually happen. The UNHCR's initiatives to deal with the environmental impact of refugee settlements are heartening; and even institutions such as the World Bank are beginning to show concern about the internal displacement threatened by large-scale infrastructural development projects, such as India's Sardar Sarovar Project on the Narmada River.[45] However, we are far from any confident optimism in this regard; and as world population keeps rising, structural inequities are being exacerbated in the age of information technology. We are left with the disturbing question, raised by forward-looking analysts such as Paul Kennedy, of whether the 'haves' can coexist with the 'have-nots'; or, as Kennedy frames it, 'How, indeed, will a technologically sophisticated, transnational, corporate culture, loyal to no government and beyond the reach of local regulation, coexist with the polyglot, hungry, and dissatisfied masses foreshadowed by a world population of nine or ten billion?'[46]

The refugee crisis and its present and future relationship to environmental problems can only be viewed from a global perspective, and this challenges conventional notions of national security. This may encourage enlightened, globalist (following Gurtov) approaches, ones that stress the humanitarian impulse. But then it may not: one can always appeal to less altruistic instincts. Ghana's Ambassador to the UN, Kofi Awoonor, was once asked how the South would be able, in times of worldwide economic constriction, to acquire sufficient development aid from the North. His answer was as blunt as it was disturbing: 'We raise up for the advantaged countries some of their big fears. Immigration is one of their fears. We say that if you don't want all of Africa on a ship coming, you have to help make conditions that allow people to stay at home.'[47] This is rather more difficult than it sounds, however, since refugees today are fleeing not only direct political persecution and war, but also a myriad of threats to their personal safety, from ecocide to female genital mutilation.

Conclusion

A minimalist definition of the term refugee is based on recognizing the political persecution of individuals who have crossed internationally recognized borders. The human rights community generally favours retaining this conventional definition, because it focuses on the political oppression that causes such movements. When determining their refugee and immigration policies, individual states are free to include other factors, such as persecution based on race or gender; and one can argue that these are also political reflections of a legitimate fear for survival.

A maximalist definition would expand the minimalist one in a number of ways. It would include those moving in search of more hospitable ground, be they in search of jobs or clean drinking water. And it might also include internal displacees, who have not crossed borders. The broadest conception would suggest that in this age of globalization, borders are becoming irrelevant and we are losing our loyalty to the nation-state, and thus we are all refugees of a sort. While I have summarily dismissed the latter interpretation, the concept of economic/environmental refugees deserves much attention today, since other factors (genocide and ecocide chief among them) have led to greater population movements than we have seen since the Second World War.

Though it is very important to stress the relationship between population movements and economic dislocation and/or environmental problems – and, further, the political nexus between them, which we have tentatively termed *ecopolitical displacement* – using the term *refugee* at this point raises several conceptual problems. It can be argued that a new legal definition would not only steal thunder from the important work being done to mitigate direct political persecution, but could also oversimplify understandings of the environmental dimension of displacement. At present, humane interventionism is very rare, and peacetime humane interventionism virtually impossible. If we were to label all those displaced by environmental problems as refugees, the internally displaced – those affected not only by desertification and landslides, but also by infrastructural projects and mining developments – would become even less visible. With regard to emergency situations of cross-border movements, precedent already exists for treating environmental refugees as legal refugees.

As for the UNHCR, it is difficult to imagine how this strained organization, even if it were expanded considerably, could deal with the greater problems of population movements. At this stage, it seems wiser to leave that body's mandate alone. This is not by any means to imply that potential host countries should not expand their own definition of refugees, or that we should ignore the sage advice of that great if somewhat idealistic humanitarian, H.G. Wells: 'Beginning with the proposition that the institutions and formulae of the future must necessarily be developed from those of the present, that one cannot start *de novo* even after a revolution; one may easily end in an attitude of excessive conservatism towards existing machinery.'[48] On the contrary, what seems needed is a reconceptualization of both development and security, one that puts human rights and the environment first and in the process seeks to retain the humanitarianism of which the human race is capable. Can this be done in an age of *globalization*? Our next and final chapter discusses that contextual term.

Though the 1999 Kosovo crisis unfolded as this book went to print, it reinforces the need of the international community to clarify our conceptions of population displacement and establish robust institutions capable of large-scale responses. It also further emphasizes the many links between state violence, ecocide, and refugees. NATO's military intervention may be viewed as a response to Serbian genocide; or it may be viewed as evidence of American resolve to continue to lead in the processes of globalization outlined in the following chapter.

5

Globalization

I've made a habit of beginning each chapter with a standard dictionary definition of the term under discussion. I will have to make an exception here because, even though *globalization* is clearly one of the most overused words in international politics today, it has yet to become part of accepted vocabulary. In the beginning of Chapter 1, I noted that – as in the past – the study of world politics today revolves around a stable of core concepts. I suggested further that while some of these are ephemera, reflecting fads of the day, others are seemingly perennial. Anarchy, diplomacy, balance of power, transnationalism, regimes: these are all concepts with which the average student of international relations must quickly become familiar in order to get hold of the literature. This book has suggested that at least three other broad concepts should be 'core' to the discipline, especially if we are to take an expanded vision of global security seriously: state violence, environmental degradation, and population displacement. These were further narrowed down to three representative terms: genocide, ecocide, and refugee. Unfortunately, both maximalist and minimalist definitions of these terms will continue to haunt those concerned with questions about sovereignty, justice, and human and environmental security.

Globalization, on the other hand, may appear more epiphenomenal than other core terms. Its popularity is testament to its ambiguity; its meaning stretches quite widely along the minimalist–maximalist spectrum, with many interpretations located somewhere (but nowhere clearly) along that line. The purpose of this chapter is twofold. First, it is intended as a conceptual discussion of the term, much as in our other chapters. Minimally, globalization refers to multilateral trade and (especially) capital liberalization and the subsequent expansion of the 'global marketplace.' This in turn refers to the post–Second World War process whereby trade barriers have been gradually reduced and domestic economies have been opened up to foreign investment. One can easily argue that this perspective, when informed by a positive assessment of the process, involves assumptions derived from a teleological neoliberalism. This position emphasizes the inevitability of the process, the subsequent wealth that it will produce, and the gradual emergence of a global middle class that will insist on a set of universal values. This latter expectation leads us to the maximalist position described below, but it is worth mentioning at this point that there is of course a critical perspective on the neoliberal agenda that counters lofty claims to progress. This leads to interpretive divisions; for example, the recent melt-down of Asian markets may be seen as indicative of a global capitalist crisis, or as a mere growing pain of the world economy.

At a more maximalist position is the idea that globalization is a process not only of expanding markets but also of continued social, technological, and political integration, moving humanity toward some sort of global civilization or even, to use an often harshly judged term, modernity. This can be seen in a positive light, or in a mixed light, or as exposing a universalist narrative justifying the dominance of a select few Western states or a transnational élite class. Regarding the last point, it is important to note that many interpret globalization as the modern term for imperialism, and see it as a process that destroys local identities and spreads capitalism to the last corners of the earth. Some even suggest that global capitalism, driven by its own 'manic logic,' is creating an inhumane world.[1] Others argue that globalization is changing our perceptions of time and space and enveloping us in a modernity or postmodernity that is redefining geopolitics. Clearly, in this chapter we will be spending more time on the maximalist perspective of globalization.

The second purpose of this chapter is to tie the term globalization to our central theme of global human security and our other discussed concepts. This is where it all comes together, since one might argue that globalization is currently setting the context in which the pursuit of security must take place. If globalization is gradually eroding the power of nation-states, then the consequences for reducing environmental damage and for contributing humanitarian assistance through government channels to refugees and others in dire need may appear bleak. On the other hand, if one accepts a positive interpretation of globalization, genocide and ecocide may be *less* likely in the future, as states because more fully integrated into an evolving global consciousness. Or, alternatively, if states come to matter less, people may come to matter more as they assert themselves against globalizing forces – a process often referred to as 'localization.'

Given its current widespread usage, one might conclude that globalization doesn't really mean anything, and that we should refrain from using the word altogether. I disagree, for two principal reasons. First, the maximalist definitions discussed below may not lead to concrete institutional measures that help those most affected, but they do stretch our imaginations, and this in itself is of pedagogical value. Second, it makes little sense to ignore the term in an era when it appears everywhere, from late-night television shows to political speeches. It is too late to put this semantic genie back in the bottle. That being said, even carefully framed interpretations of the term can cover far too much ground to be useful. For example, James Rosenau writes that 'any technological, psychological, social, economic, or political developments that foster the expansion of interests and practises beyond established boundaries are both sources and expressions of the processes of globalization, just as any developments in these realms that limit or reduce interests are both sources and expressions of localizing processes.'[2]

While I retain great respect for Rosenau's innovative contributions to the field of international relations, this statement would make even a maximalist definition seem restrictive. If globalization – or its opposite, localization (as offered by Rosenau and others) – means everything, it means very little.

Part of the dilemma in defining this term is that definitions are so assumptive regarding whether or not the process being described is actually taking place. So there are two questions here: What is globalization? And is it occurring? We can say with some confidence that the global marketplace has expanded and that interdependence has been the result; it is another matter altogether to assert that the concrete manifestations of the maximalist conceptions of globalization, involving (for example) the establishment of universal values or the emergence of global technology, are actually occurring.

Trade and Investment Liberalization

The adjective *global* has long been a popular one in the literature on international relations. There have been several variants of globalism, including the 'humanist globalism' mentioned in the last chapter. As well, the term has been used more analytically by those who have opposed a realist ontology and preferred some sort of systems conception of the international system.[3] Two decades ago, Albert Bergensen wrote of a general, and gradual, shift from utilitarianism to globology, or 'the shift from the individual to the world as a whole as the primordial unit of analysis.'[4] The same year, Rosenau wrote of the 'transnationalization of world politics,' whereby state–state interaction had been 'supplemented by relations among private individuals, groups and societies.'[5] Even before this, Marshal McLuhan popularized the idea of a *global village*, linked by electronic communication. What is new, it can be argued, is the frequency with which the term globalization has been employed by both proponents and critics of the neoliberal perspective.

The minimalist definition of globalization would refer simply to trade and capital liberalization, which expands what neoliberals call the 'global marketplace.' In this context, globalization involves states taking steps to reduce impediments to international trade; to this end, nations negotiate for lower tariffs, less intrusive mercantilist policies, and greater freedom for capital to cross international borders. Alan Tonelson defines globalization as 'the increasing integration of international markets being brought about by rapidly expanding worldwide flows of goods, services, capital, information, and sometimes people' (note the qualifying 'sometimes' before the term people).[6] We might sneak in some assumptions dominant in neoliberal discourse, such as the idea that trade is an inherently good thing, despite the difficult adjustments required within economies, because it lessens the propensity for war while increasing the ability of states to gain wealth. Naturally, private property rights (physical and intellectual) are a factor here as well. But what is really happening, according to this perspective, is that previously confining borders are being opened, which is the natural extension of multilateral co-operation since the signing of the General Agreement on Tariffs and Trade (GATT) in the late 1940s.

A minimalist perspective would argue, then, that globalization is simply an economic process; adopting slightly harsh terms, we might call this perspective one of blinkered neoliberalism. Many of the maximalists discussed below, writing from a political economy perspective, would agree that an economic process is at work; even so, the neoliberal view remains enmeshed in classical economists' predisposition to dissociate the political from the economic in any but a benign manner. It is accepted that globalization is a rising tide against which only the foolhardy would offer serious resistance. Governments can and should do their best to steer economies along, but at the same time they should promote the lifting of trade barriers and the opening of the global marketplace. (Naturally, this is especially the case for countries that depend heavily on foreign trade, and this includes most countries today).[7] Recent fiscal crises in Asia notwithstanding, the export-led development model is accepted as the most efficient manner by which states in the South can replicate the development experience of the North.

There is little new in this, of course. One could argue that the only significant differences are that advances in telecommunications have been given a pivotal causal role (and that telecommunications firms and other Internet-related industries are major actors), and that we have a new and sexy term to use. The old policies advocated by the West's private and public financial institutions – market primacy, low social-spending levels, reduced state regulation, privatization – are still there, and so is the old canon about comparative advantage being derived from production and distribution tailored to market specialization. Implicit in this definition is the notion that the state is losing some authority on the world stage, but this is neither lamented nor closely analyzed: Like so many things with regard to globalization, it just *is*. States are assumed to be 'relegated to the role of facilitators in the adaptation of the national economy to the new realities of emerging international economic structures ... to creating the policy environment, both nationally and internationally, which favours the globalization of production and service industries.'[8] According to this perspective, multilateral forums such as the G–7 and the OECD (Organization for Economic Cooperation and Development) serve this function.

According to a minimalist, neoliberal perspective, the greatest threat to globalization is not a postmodernist rush toward localizing forces, but a parochiality inherent in regional, as opposed to global, economic co-operation. The push toward freer global trade is continuing with the conclusion of the GATT Uruguay Round. The World Trade Organization (WTO) has effectively replaced the GATT Secretariat in Geneva. A biannual ministerial meeting will dictate the WTO's direction, and this council will have subsidiary working bodies specializing in areas of trade such as goods, services, the environment, and intellectual property. Countries accused of unfair trading practices will have to answer to the council, and other states will be permitted to impose countervailing sanctions and to receive whatever compensation the WTO panel deems appropriate. This is a big step, when one considers that GATT outcomes were often ignored. One might argue that the WTO represents the subordination of national sovereignty to an international organization which is not accountable to the citizens of individual states. Given the apparent strength of this new institution (to which states such as Russia and China are eager to belong), and given the shift toward a market-based world economy that is producing the effect of globalization described earlier, one might think that a truly global liberal trading order is emerging. Or is it? Protectionism still exists, though it may in some cases be disguised; and a number of regional organizations are setting their own precedents. Chief among these is the European Union.

However, we should be very careful about using the EU as a prototype for future regionalism. In fact it is a common criticism of the neofunctionalist school that the embryonic standard it used – that of the European Community – simply isn't exportable elsewhere. Europe has a very high standard of living (though there are differences within the region that the EU is supposed to attempt to rectify); it has global connections in both trade and diplomacy; and it has had the military protection of the United States. Clearly, the EU should be seen as a unique situation, and other free trade agreements, such as the North American Free Trade Agreement, are not intended to induce the same level of economic and political integration (though NAFTA's more vocal Canadian critics argue that it will ultimately have this effect).

At the same time, we *can* argue that there is a noticeable trend toward regional integration in trade and investment, and toward the creation of political mechanisms to facilitate this. We could well have a free trade area from Alaska to Argentina by the year 2005. The Pacific nations could become more closely integrated by that time, with Japan and China vying as regional leaders and the ASEAN states forming a bloc. And Europe's integration, both economic and political, will probably continue. This suggests a possible triregional model of the future world economy: the Americas, Asia, and Europe (with Eastern Europe, Russia, and Africa connected, though unlikely to be made prosperous). Ultimately, these three fortresses will congeal into political units that will confront each other over the world's remaining resources. Some see all of this as the only alternative to a more liberal global trading order, and such a model contrasts in style and (ultimately) purpose with the more global approach encouraged by GATT and the newly established WTO. Those who argue that peace follows commerce might do well to consider whether dividing the world into three large trade zones will encourage a tripolar mentality that could even lead to military conflict as the interests of the three areas begin to conflict.

Some of globalization's proponents, however, would argue that regional integration is just a step along the road to a harmonized global economy – that it occurs simultaneously as the world economy develops, and that the two processes reinforce rather than challenge each other, and that as regional organizations form, the political machinery of multilateralism will be created. It has become almost habitual among students of international political economy to refer to the European Union as the prime example of regional neofunctionalism, but there are other regions where states are engaging in multilateralism based on regional affiliation. A famous example, of course, is NAFTA, which presently includes Canada, the United States, and Mexico, and which may soon include several Latin American countries as well. NAFTA has served as the basis for the emerging Multilateral Agreement on Investment, or MAI, negotiated through the OECD secretariat in Paris.

However, the MAI has not come into being, contrary to the expectations of the state leaders who initiated discussion about it. The agreement would limit the ability of signatory governments to treat foreign investors differently from domestic investors. This is, of course, quite significant, since an important aspect of state sovereignty has been the ability of states to dictate policy to foreign investors. Critics claim this reduces the role played by democratic institutions in passing legislation. Others argue that it compromises the ability of states to protect culture from foreign intrusion. The nongovernmental community lobbied hard against the MAI, linking it to the general evils of globalization. But much of the opposition to the agreement has come from states themselves, which are still reluctant to sacrifice too much sovereignty too soon, at a time when the displacement caused by a globalizing economy remains a warm (if not always hot) political issue.

Nonetheless, seen in the minimalist light, globalization is usually cast as a progressive, productive stage in the evolution of world commerce, akin to the great transformations that followed the liberalization of trade in medieval Europe. However, progress and productivity are at best relative concepts. Economic dislocation typically follows market liberalization. We should not forget that borders have been slowly opening to trade for many years, and that as a result certain sectors of the population have suffered while others have prospered. Ethan Kapstein reminds us of this in a discussion of the 1846 British decision to lift the Corn Laws. He refers to this as a policy 'consciously designed to globalize the economy in favor of specific interests.'[9] Manchester factory owners needed more cheap labour, and what better way to attain it than by opening up the British market to staple agricultural imports, forcing small farm owners and workers off the land and into the cities as prices dropped? The revolt in Chiapas, Mexico, as NAFTA came into effect may be seen as a response to similarly damaging policies. The renowned Canadian international political economist Robert Cox argues that the analysis of the 'globalization thrust' must ultimately begin with an understanding of the 'internationalization of production. The internationalizing process results when capital considers the productive resources of the world as a whole and locates elements of complex globalized production systems at points of greatest cost advantage. The critical factor is information on how most profitably to combine components in that production process ... Producing units take advantage of abundant, cheap, and malleable labour where it is to be found, and of robotization where it is not.'[10]

This materialist perspective serves as a counteranalysis to the minimalist neoliberal perspective; it also points the way to a maximalist understanding of globalization as a process of worldwide imperialism.

The minimalist, neoliberal perspective sees globalization today as a pretty good thing. Though there is little direct attention paid to the social, environmental, and even political repercussions of opening borders, it is assumed that the long-term effects will be positive and will lead to the creation of a global middle class. Even former strategic analysts are coming to this conclusion. Gwen Dwyer, for example, writes: 'What is actually happening in the world now is akin to what happened in Europe at the end of the feudal era. A new class is emerging, a global middle class, and it will ultimately come to dominate global society both numerically and economically ... The [1996] UNDP report was an extended whine on familiar old themes. It depicted poor countries as the norm, and blamed their poverty on the rich ones ... The report's authors were probably being manipulative rather than just plain ignorant, for it is their job to drum up sympathy and help for the world's poor.'[11]

Dwyer argues that the overall statistics on economic growth and human welfare have been skewed by the 'African disaster.' Leaving aside the obvious point that we had better not ignore the African disaster (for moral as well as analytic reasons!), Dwyer's account is based on a global acceptance of the standards and values of this new middle class, this globalizing cosmopolitan semi-élite. A global consumer society will emerge, and the irrationality of counterhegemonic inclinations will finally be exposed by marketplace dynamics. This moves us toward a maximalist perspective, which suggests that globalization is ultimately a process of social and political convergence on an unprecedented (and ultimately universal) scale.

Social, Technological, and Political Convergence

Perhaps the most succinct definition of globalization, and one of the more widely quoted, is offered by Malcolm Waters in his short but fascinating book on the topic. As a sociologist, Waters is more interested in the relationships inherent in global shifts; and he defines globalization as a 'social process in which the constraints of geography on social and cultural arrangements recede and in which people become increasingly aware that they are receding.'[12]

Waters believes that globalization, as we conceive of it currently, is but another stage of a continuous (if not necessarily teleological) historical process, one that has emerged from the 'fits and starts of various ancient imperial expansions, pillaging and trading oceanic explorations, and the spread of religious ideas.' This process was interrupted by the European Middle Ages, a period of 'inward-looking territorialism'; but then picked up again during the fifteenth and sixteenth centuries, when the Copernican Revolution convinced humanity that it occupied a globe (rather than a flat, endless plain), and when European expansion took the ideas that today still shape the global economy – market-based trade, for example – to distant lands where people previously lived in 'virtually complete ignorance of each other's existence.'[13] As time passes, people are driven by the search for wealth or security to make new connections with others, and from those connections emerge new understandings about ourselves and our distance from others. This is at heart a cognitive process.

Globalization, then, is immediately conceived as more than an economic process: its roots, and its implications, are inherently social. The proximity that technology affords leads to social commonality, if not sameness. This position stops short of suggesting that we are heading toward an undifferentiated social and political system, but it does suggest that values and ideas are spread through contact and that this will ultimately have a profound impact on how we see the world and interact with others in it. The icons of western culture, from commercial slogans to liberal democracy, have made their way around the globe. But throughout history, art and culture have always been influenced by outsiders' symbols and artifacts. These are spread through various mechanisms, from word-of-mouth to the printing press to the Internet; the medium is communicative technology, which advances in periodic leaps through common events such as warfare, religious crusade, or commercial innovation.

Some argue that globalization is best seen as a technological process; these arguments either border on or embrace technological determinism. Sociologists have introduced a *convergence theory* which implies that the 'opportunities and demands presented by modern technology promote the convergence of all societies toward a single set of social patterns and individual behaviours.'[14] In other words, the adoption of Western technology and science will lead to the establishment of political institutions and cultural environments similar to those in the 'advanced' European/American worlds. Thus, in rather teleological style, the argument follows that globalization will inevitably be realized through technological standardization.[15] This echoes some of the earlier technocratic arguments favoured by functionalists and others.

However, such a postulation leaves a great deal of room for healthy speculation. One might point to the evolutionary spread of capitalism, or to the spread of neoliberal precepts, as the source of this convergence; the technology employed was but a means to the result. We might add that such a theory dismisses the potential political impact, and viability, of counterhegemonic movements. There are obvious cases where a distaste for Western society has led to an assertion of anti-Western political change, such as the Iranian Revolution that ushered into power the late Ayatollah Khomeini. But in the more general sense, one can argue that culture does not necessarily converge simply because of technological similarities. There are distinct patterns of social interaction within different societies. Japan, the United States, and Germany all have adopted similar industrial technologies, yet they remain culturally quite different. And though many would argue with this, we can even point to significant cultural differences between countries as similar in technological circumstances as the United States and Canada.

James Rosenau argues that technology has 'profoundly altered the scale on which human affairs take place, allowing people to do more things in less time and with wider repercussions than could have been imagined in earlier eras.'[16] At the same time, technological advances will be jealously guarded in a world still full of competitive states. As two international political economists conclude, technology's 'critical nature has led to restrictions, sanctions, thievery, and espionage, all of which prohibit the free flow and testing of ideas ... In the area of technology, prevalent notions among advanced states seem to be more mercantilist than a liberal economic philosophy.'[17] If technology is the grand spreader, then it may in fact be restricted in its duty by the harsh realities of economic competition.

Political geographers have also seized on the idea of time-space compression encouraged by advances in transportation and communication technology.[18] Distance declines in importance, and the pace of consumption is accelerated by the mobilization of mass marketing and the advent of the service economy. This is encouraged by the rise of credit as the fundamental means of business transaction, the electronic linkage of stock-buyers and sellers around the world, and the opportunity of daily intercontinental transportation. One might argue further that the Internet provides a similar travelling experience for the masses, though it is a virtual experience at best, and one that is limited to those who enjoy access to the relevant technology – still a small minority. Furthermore, global cities such as New York, London, and Tokyo can be conceived as 'centres of interpretation,' capitalizing on the spatial proximity of knowledge.[19] Again, this is nothing substantially novel, though it is a fascinating play on the core–periphery theme. John Allen and Chris Hamnett offer this succinct summary: 'The reordering of distance, the overcoming of spatial barriers, the shortening of time-horizons, and the ability to link distant populations in a more immediate and intense manner, are prerequisites of global talk ... [However] the world is neither shrinking for everyone, nor is it of positive benefit to all those caught up in the maelstrom.'[20]

And yet there is no escape, since information is now a 'basic resource needed for technico-economic activity, on a par with matter and energy.'[21] Most would have to acknowledge this, even as it affects those less integrated in the world economy. As such, some sectors of society will prosper, while those marginalized from evolving levels of access to this resource will only become poorer. The next generation of complex technology 'required' to run the core areas of the world economy will no doubt increase wealth and opportunity for those with access to the requisite education. We must keep in mind, however, that we live in a world where, despite years of literacy programs, over one billion adults still cannot read or write, and over 100 million children of primary school age are not able to attend school every year.[22] Furthermore, we must also ask ourselves whether invaluable local knowledge is being wasted in the rush toward international standardization.[23] If it is – and it certainly has been throughout the history of Western expansionism – this may be one of the most pertinent threats to human and global security we collectively face.

In terms of the political corollary of all this technical and social change, we see little clear evidence that the nation-state is receding as the fundamental political unit in the world system. It is in fact deeply entrenched both in citizens' lives and in international affairs. The UN, as we've mentioned in previous chapters, has limited power to intervene in the affairs of states; it has an ongoing financial and even legitimacy crisis on its hands; and in the vast majority of cases it simply cannot replace the state as an effective supplier of basic needs. Indeed, some critical theorists argue that international organizations can at best supply 'global poor relief and riot control'[24] in an effort to maintain the very exploitive system that causes poverty and social unrest. We will return to this theme soon.

Finally, many argue instead that the spread of Western culture has accompanied the spread of Western capitalism. According to this critical perspective, it is not a matter of the best values and technologies rising to the top as comparisons take place and people ostensibly vote with their feet. It is, rather, a matter of imposition. The neoliberal variant may in fact be the contemporary equivalent of what development theorists at one time referred to as *modernization*. The latter term was harshly criticized because it implied that only Western states were modern and that those developing states which had failed to reach the point of being mass consumption societies were backward, perhaps because of geography and also because of cultural or even personality traits prevalent in their societies. Thus, one might argue that the pressure to globalize, to become even further involved with the world economy and its regimes, is a destructive one, with its implication that non-Western societies have no choice, if they wish to be 'with it,' other than to adopt the conventional attributes of the West: capitalism, commercial culture, secular governance, and a secular emphasis on the 'here and now.'[25]

Globalization, then, may be looked at as a process that has been in effect for many centuries and that involves the spread of both ideas and capital, for both good and bad. Whether we believe this is about to result in a newly christened global society, or already has, depends on whether we take the next step in the maximalist conceptual sphere. At the extreme maximalist end of the conceptual spectrum, globalization represents an age of universalism, when the convergence described above becomes all-embracing. The globe is increasingly looking like a single marketplace with rules and co-operative efforts that make a standard out of the neoliberal model. Or, in a more negative light, the globe is increasingly looking like a Western-dominated imperialist system that has already soaked up whatever futile resistance was offered in years past. Both these descriptions verge on caricature, as well decried by Philip Cerny.[26] But it is worth noting that the caricature comes from both left and right – from those opposed to free trade agendas and from those in favour. Ironically, it is a unifying concept at this level, though the two sides begin from utterly different normative assumptions.

Again, there are two questions here: Is such an all-encompassing conception of the term globalization warranted? Its name certainly suggests it is. And is such a thing really happening? It is clear that the processes described above are taking shape – marketplace expansion and social and political convergence – but are we really on the road to a globalized society? Among many others, political scientist Jorge Nef believes that a truly global society has never existed:

> What does exist is a social construction: an image of social interactions encapsulated in terms such as the global village and similar allegories. There is, however, a process of globalisation, expressed in an increased velocity of elite circulation and communications across national boundaries conveying and strengthening that image ... For most of the world population, despite claims of an emerging cosmopolitanism, the globalisation of social life means hardly more than the virtual reality of canned media and the advertising of products.[27]

One can certainly exaggerate the presence and, especially, the impact of a global trend when it is assumed to be in its infancy. But globalization survives as ideology today; it is consciously accepted and employed as such by governments, including the current political leadership in Washington and Ottawa. Robert Cox suggests that it underpins a 'transnational process of consensus formation' that 'generates consensual guidelines ... that are transmitted into the policy-making channels of national governments and big corporations.'[28]

Though Robert Walker encourages us to think beyond the 'celebratory teleologies of modern political life within the great universalizing particular, the modern state,' it may be the great universalizing universal, the modern global, that is most celebrated today.[29] Yet surely a universalistic conception of globalization belittles the strong cultural differences that still, thankfully, exist. For example, one author argues that the world is still fundamentally divided into at least eight civilizational systems: the Chinese, Hindu, Islamic, Japanese, Latin American syncretist, Islamic, non-Islamic African, and Christian.[30] Does a secular vision of globalization, based on markets and investment and common values, do justice to the inherent diversity of humanity? What about the major split, presented as axiomatic by some analysts, between the Eastern and Western or Islamic and Christian communities? What about the differences within every nation-state, between rich and poor, between ethnic groups, between male and female? In short, what about human diversity and, for that matter, environmental diversity as well? At the very least we can suggest that the impact of Western intrusion will vary between societies; it would be grossly simplistic to anticipate a standard response, be it acceptive or confrontational.

Examining the idea that globalization will produce some sort of global culture, Randall White asks: 'Just what could some authentic global culture possibly be? To take just the most obvious point, how would it deal with the at once simple but highly complex fact that in the world at large today we do not all speak anything like the same language? In the face of such monumental questions ... globalization ideology as a practical matter can only fall back on something that bears a close resemblance to the old imperialism that really did exist, but that the world at large now rightly regards as too repugnant for the future.'[31]

Critics would argue that what is perhaps most pernicious about the globalization idea – if it is taken from a maximalist perspective without regard for counterhegemonic potential – is that it suggests that some superior force is at work driving us all toward convergence along the Western model. It is common for corporate executives, and politicians, and teenagers flipping hamburgers, to talk of globalization as if it were inevitable, and as if those who do not succumb to its tide will lose out in the future. If this fatalism is justified, then there is little use even thinking about setting alternative courses, and we must grudgingly accept the fact that many people will be harmed by the process as others gain. The author of a recent report on the UN Human Development Index believes that a 'new vision of global solidarity is needed to match the push for globalization. Without this vision and action, globalization will become a monster of gargantuan excesses and grotesque inequalities.'[32] Many would argue that the monster is already upon us.

Globalization, Sovereignty, and International Organization

Throughout this book we've returned to the theme of sovereignty in global politics, to the resilience of the nation-state and the principle of nonintervention. In all the threats to human and environmental security identified here – genocide, ecocide, the rising tide of refugees – states play a key role. The neoliberal and critical perspectives on globalization tend to paint the state, respectively, as a nuisance in the way of progress, or as an accomplice in an imperialist project. In much of the literature on the globalizing economy, the state is regarded either as a done deal or as a declining entity with a serious identity crisis. A quickly famous example was the following passage from Robert Reich, former Secretary of Labour to the Clinton Administration: 'As almost every factor of production – money, technology, factories, and equipment – moves effortlessly across borders, the very idea of an American economy is becoming meaningless, as are the notions of an American corporation, American capital, American products, and American technology. A similar transformation is affecting every other nation.'[33]

It is a short step from this to acceptance of the idea that we are either living in or entering a truly borderless world, where territorial limits are maintained for largely demonstrative purposes (or to keep military establishments alive) and the real work of the world economy gets done through the dynamics of an international marketplace. Future human activity will be to some extent determined by the process of interacting with the global economy and reacting to long-term and/or violent changes within that economy. If we accept the maxim that the state is thus doomed to obsolescence, it is not clear whether it serves any purpose to discuss the institutional implications of our definition of globalization. When it comes to the nation-state, adherents to most of the maximalist positions discussed in this text would argue that that institution has been the major stumbling block toward a more humane world – that, in other words, the state must go. But where will it go? One can certainly suggest that governments will lose their ability to set policies that fly in the face of global economic competition; but this is some way from suggesting that they will be impotent in all matters. And they will turn to international institutions for assistance as well.

In the past the nation-state has been viewed as a terrible invention dividing humanity and providing a systemic context for war. Ironically, the question we face today is whether the preservation of the nation-state as a potential unilateral actor is not, in fact, a worthwhile objective. If globalization is a threat to individuality and may promote some of the less desirable attributes of large-scale change (population movements, environmental destruction, and so on), we may end up defending the state and its right, or obligation, to take unilateral action to protect its citizens from the potential ravages of the global economy. It may sound too stark a dichotomy – a world ruled by states, or one ruled by corporations – but do we want to take a chance with the latter, even if it means ridding the world of the territorial imperatives of statehood?

It is certainly true that states have been keeping pace with globalization through the gradual acceptance of supralateral agreements like the WTO, which puts decision-making power in the hands of international arbitrators. We should be clear, however, that selective supralateralism does not world government make. Again, the will to end the life of the state system because of the problems it has created for international security and progress in some issue-areas seems to be getting sapped by the realization that vast amounts of multilateral activity, at the state level, are in fact necessary to make a nonstate-based world possible in the long run. Even significant and disruptive unilateral actions, such as breaking with the freedom-of-the-seas legal tradition to seize destructive fishing vessels, will sometimes be necessary as well.[34] Interestingly, a shift seems to be occurring in the old pro-state and anti-state coalitions that developed in international relations theory during the Cold War: even Richard Falk now warns us of the danger of 'demonizing state and market forces and of romanticizing an emergent global civil society' (498–9). Functionalism, meanwhile, has come to represent technocratic romanticism, itself one of the causes of the current environmental crises.

One might argue that the academic world, post-neofunctionalism, has turned instead to a lighter if much more filling substitute, known tentatively as *global policy studies*, mentioned briefly in Chapter 1. We can describe this self-defined academic territory as 'the study of international interactions designed to deal with shared public policy problems,' like transboundary issues, common property dilemmas, and 'simultaneous problems,' such as health, education, and welfare, 'about which all countries can learn from each other.'[35] According to Marvin Soroos this involves a threefold emphasis: on a rational policy process (in other words, on a steady if occasionally interrupted stream of policy formation, from the recognition of problems to the evaluation of policy); an understanding of the overall political systems involved (a sort of plural structural functionalism); and the study of regulations (prohibitions, limits, obligations, standards, privileges).[36]

As governments grapple with external pressures, and are pressured by élites to preserve certain privileges while discarding others, they feel an obligation to pursue policy co-ordination. While it is obvious that transborder environmental problems can push governments in this direction, other issue-areas are less pushy. Migration policies have recently fallen into the crack of intergovernmental policy co-ordination as Northern nations continue to tighten their borders or move closer to rich-only admittance policies. Policy co-ordination on everything from anti–drug smuggling efforts to the protection of rare tortoises is in effect, though it is of course quite debatable whether or not governmental enthusiasm for these multilateral initiatives is the result of current public pressure or longer-term commitments. There are also some serious questions as to just how 'deep' this type of policy co-ordination can really go, given the many complications and unexpected events that colour the domestic and international political landscape.

A critical perspective will tend to reject policy co-ordination, and multilateralism in general, as a form of hegemonic managerialism, and one that is doomed in an age of mutual vulnerability. Policy co-ordination either puts off the inevitable obsolescence of the state by softly guiding the neoliberal agenda, or perpetuates inherently unjust social relations by propping the state up and justifying its reach. Jorge Nef argues that the periphery's problems will eventually hit home, despite the best managerial efforts of the core (conceived as a transnational class of élites, and not as any particular state or states): 'Harmony and predictability at the level of the transnational core does not necessarily translate into security at the base. As production, finance and distribution in a rapidly globalizing economy become transnationalized, so does mass economic vulnerability. After the years of widespread prosperity during the sixties and the seventies, instability and exposure have become endemic.'[37]

The state will survive globalization, and in fact many states are currently driving it with their rapid promotion of the minimalist perspective described earlier. If we are heading toward a

Western-oriented global culture and economy, there is no need to assume that the contemporary state cannot adjust and serve this broader purpose. The operative question seems to be whether the state can provide security to those who will be most threatened by the process, and here the answer seems at present a mixed one. States will protect dominant élites from the ravages of the global marketplace – to a point. It is less clear whether those most susceptible to change – deindustrialized factory workers, those involved in the extraction of depleted resources, those with minimal personal resources to cope with change – will be similarly protected.

Conclusion

I have looked in some depth at five interconnected terms in this book: security, genocide, ecocide, refugee, and globalization. I have contrasted minimalist with maximalist conceptions of each of them, and tried to explore some of their many implications. In almost every case, for the sake of applicability, I favour the minimalist definition. The maximalist definitions are of great value in that they challenge convention and force us to look critically at the state and modern society (including the international community) in general. However, I am cautious about advocating their repeated use, in the classroom or anywhere else, because of the ambiguity they engender.

This is acutely evident when we discuss operationalizing the maximalist definitions in the institutional sense. We have no global authority that can prevent genocide according to the Convention, let alone according to Henry Shue. The price of creating one might be unacceptable, not only to entrenched state élites but also to those subjugated under any new global power. We have no way of effectively outlawing ecocide during warfare, let alone of forcing a green economy on the world. And as for refugees, the concept of political refuge is a vital one and we are far from seeing states change their refugee determination policies to include broader categories (though there is room for considerable navigation within the political refugee category). These statements are not intended to invoke defeatism on the part of those actively campaigning, within and without the state system, to save humanity from these scourges, but rather to keep things in earned perspective.

With globalization, however, I am tempted to accept the maximalist vision as the more appropriate one, because it is not a term that is subject to extant definition by international law, and because the minimalist definition – that globalization is simply about expanding investment and trading opportunities – does injustice to the inherent (and historical) politics of the process. While I reject the rosy teleological premise of the neoliberal perspective outlined above, globalization is something bigger than its many parts. In a limited fashion, we are heading toward convergence, albeit at different speeds and with different obstacles in the way. (Much as Malcolm Waters suggests, there is nothing new about this except what we choose to call it.) One of those obstacles, according to the neoliberal agenda, is difference. (This raises a crisis of theoretical legitimacy, since the neoliberal agenda is premised on individuality yet promotes homogenization.) Therefore, political control of individual communities must be, and *is* being, usurped by a global corporate élite. This is a brash statement; however, it indicates a direction, not an arrived-at place.

It will be vital to counter this trend if we are to retain a true vision of human and environmental *security*. Globalization will have mixed effects, of course, but it will certainly create great insecurity for many who simply don't want to, or cannot, go along for the ride. And all the issue-areas that activists and academics have worked so hard to bring into the realm of open debate – such as environmentalism, human rights, gender equality, and the preservation of indigenous cultures and peoples – could be swiped away by the grander neoliberal project. That some values should be universal remains a fundamental conviction for most of us; the obligation of states and other collectivities to avoid committing genocide and ecocide, and to avoid mistreating refugees, could be key here. But this does not necessitate the blanket absorption of a Western conception of human rights, nor, for that matter, the universal desire for Western consumption levels.

Conclusion

In the belief that a major part of understanding is in the act of definition, this book has explored the meaning of several terms that are representative of severe threats to human and global security in the post–Cold War era. Unfortunately, these terms will remain with us into the next century, and we (as citizens, academics, policymakers, and others) will struggle to respond to them. In order to do so we need to explore the conceptual implications of contrasting interpretations of meaning, and this book has attempted to provide such a background discussion.

In each case we contrasted a minimalist definition, focused primarily on a narrow legal definition of a term, with a maximalist definition, which emphasized the broader sociopolitical implications of the term under consideration. In the case of security, a minimalist conception would limit us to the act of protecting states from external attack. A maximalist definition would encompass, besides transboundary threats, intranational threats to human security caused by ethnic conflict, civil war, oppression, and other factors. This led to a discussion of four factors I consider to be essential to our understanding of contemporary global and human security: state violence, environmental degradation, population displacement, and, finally, globalization itself.

The chart below covers the essential ground of the terms we have already discussed in detail. For each term there is a broadening of the concept, in terms of its causes and impact, as we

Terminological Spectra

MINIMALIST		MAXIMALIST
	Genocide	
Persecution of select groups	State negligence	Effect of modern society
	Ecocide	
Environmental warfare	Military preparation	Industrialization/ overconsumption
	Refugee	
Politically persecuted border-crossers	Those fleeing social conditions across borders	Economic/environmental refugees, internal and international
	Globalization	
Trade and capital liberalization	Political/social convergence	Universalism/ imperialism
	Security	
Of nation-states, from military attack	Of other collectivities, from other varied threats	Global human and environmental

move from left to right. The connection between minimalist and maximalist conceptions of our terms should not be seen as linear, however. To some extent the concepts soften as they broaden; that is, they lose analytic and legal precision. As a practical matter, then, we should stress the minimalist conceptions when addressing institutional responses to the questions of genocide, ecocide, and refugee movements. But the terms *globalization* and *security* don't mean as much in their minimalist conceptions; here, the opposite end of the spectrum is more illustrative of the processes taking shape today in global politics.

This brings us back to our first term, security itself. Here again, I am inclined to accept the maximalist conception, since security for one state, or one empire, or one group of élites, is an impossible dream in this age of mutual vulnerability; and since it is necessary to look both beyond and within states to properly identify the threats facing humanity today. Rather than an overwhelmed defeatism, what emerges from this study is a renewed sense of the need to examine core concepts in world politics, and to continue the fight against threats to human and nonhuman life. By speaking out against genocide and ecocide, and by advocating refugee relief, we can contribute toward a more humane and secure world; by maintaining a critical perspective on globalization, we can continue to identify the other threats to human and global security which this new age is bringing upon us.

The maximalist definitions of these terms suggest that conventional understandings are inadequate; they also imply that our entire understanding of international relations, which is based mainly on state–state interactions and diplomacy, is insufficient. Of course, many international relations theorists have been arguing this for decades, but the point seems more self-evident now than it has ever been. This is why the maximalist perspectives offer rich pedagogical material. Though minimalist perspectives can lead to more concrete institutional suggestions (and can teach students much about international law), there remains the need to think about the broader meaning of the concepts they employ.

This book has covered much ground, but there is far more to be covered. The new security agenda shifts our focus away from bilateral superpower conflict and implores us to consider genuine threats to human and global security. I have identified four: genocide, ecocide, refugee generation, and globalization. These are some of the epic threats of our time, and we will be remiss as scholars and/or activists if we don't seriously consider the implications of how we, personally, define these contestable terms. But there are others, of course, and much more work to do.

Notes

Chapter 1.   Technology and Security in World Politics

1 R.E. Allen, ed., *The Oxford Dictionary of Current English* (Oxford: Oxford University Press, 1986), 23.

2 For a classic discussion, see Kenneth Waltz, *Man, the State, and War: A Theoretical Analysis* (New York: Columbia University Press, 1959). This anarchic system was Waltz' 'third image' of world politics, and he would build on the theme with later, *structural realist* work, most importantly *Theory of International Politics* (Reading, MA: Addison-Wesley, 1979).

3 Hedley Bull, *The Anarchical Society: A Study of Order in World Politics* (London: Macmillan, 1977), 13.

4 On this, the definitive work is Robert Gilpin's *War and Change in World Politics* (Cambridge: Cambridge University Press, 1981).

5 For a recent compilation of essays related to the regime concept, see Volker Rittberger, ed., *Regime Theory and International Relations* (Oxford: Clarendon Press, 1993). Rittberger writes of the European use of the concept as 'The Adaptive Internalization of an American Social Science Concept,' and indeed, it originated when some prominent American scholars pursued the question; see S. Krasner, ed., *International Regimes* (Ithaca, NY: Cornell University Press, 1983). See also J. Rosenau and E-O Czempiel, eds., *Governance without Government: Order and Change in World Politics* (Cambridge: Cambridge University Press, 1992); and Steven Weber, 'Institutions and Change,' in M. Doyle and J. Ikenberry, eds., *New Thinking in International Relations Theory* (Boulder, CO: Westview, 1997), 229–65.

6 'The Balance of Power: Prescription, Concept or Propaganda?' *World Politics* 5 (1953), 442–77.

7 For an interesting and recent treatment of the term, see Jens Bartelson, *A Genealogy of Sovereignty* (Cambridge: Cambridge University Press, 1995).

8 John Ruggie, 'Multilateralism: The Anatomy of an Institution,' in same; and H. Milner, ed., *Multilateralism Matters: New Directions in World Politics* (New York: Columbia University Press, 1993), 3–47. This volume, which is derived from the Ford Foundation Workshop on Multilateralism, is probably the most important book on international institutions since S. Krasner, ed., *International Regimes* (Ithaca, NY: Cornell, 1983). See also Robert Keohane, 'Multilateralism: An Agenda for Research,' *International Journal* 15:4 (1990), 731–64.

9 Stuart Nagel, 'Introduction,' in same, ed., *Global Policy Studies: International Interaction toward Improving Public Policy* (New York: St. Martin's, 1991), xiii.

10 *American Hegemony and the Trilateral Commission* (Cambridge: Cambridge University Press, 1990), 1.

11 See, for example, Robert Johansen, 'Building World Security: The Need for Strengthened International Institutions,' in M. Klare and D. Thomas, eds., *World Security: Challenges for a New Century*, Second Edition (New York: St. Martin's, 1994), 372–97.

12 Readers with a background in the endless debates concerning international relations theory will enjoy reading the amusing and often profound series of plays in James Rosenau, ed., *Global Voices: Dialogues in International Relations* (Boulder, CO: Westview Press, 1993).

13 See Jim George, *Discourses of Global Politics: A Critical (Re)Introduction to International Relations* (Boulder, CO: Lynne Rienner, 1994). Of course, this debate is hardly limited, or even new to, international relations as a discipline. See, for example, S. Aronwitz, *Science as Power: Discourse and Ideology in Modern Society* (Minneapolis: University of Minnesota Press, 1988).

14 Parts of this discussion are from 'The Environmental Enlightenment: Security Analysis Meets Ecology,' in *Coexistence: A Review of East-West and Development Issues* 31 (1994), 127–46.

15 Still cited as the formative text in American world politics studies is Hans Morgenthau's *Politics among Nations: The Struggle for Power and Peace* (New York: Alfred Knopf, 1950).

16 For the central debate, from a largely American perspective, see C. Kegley, ed., *Controversies in International Relations Theory: Realism and the Neoliberal Challenge* (New York: St. Martin's Press, 1995).

17 'World Interests and the Changing Dimensions of Security,' in Klare and Thomas, eds., *World Security*, 10–26.

18 A recent example of the former is the book edited by J. Brecher, J. Brown Childs, and J. Cutler, *Global Visions: Beyond the New World Order* (Montreal: Black Rose, 1993); and of the latter, C.T. Sjolander and W. Cox, eds., *Beyond Positivism: Critical Reflections on International Relations* (Boulder, CO: Lynne

Rienner, 1994). See also R. Maghroori and B. Ramberg, *Globalism versus Realism: International Relations Third Debate* (Boulder, CO: Westview, 1982); and Lynn Miller, *Global Order: Values and Power in International Politics* (Boulder, CO: Westview, 1985). Finally, for an excellent if already outdated discussion that explores divergent theoretical paths, see Kal Holsti, 'Mirror, Mirror on the Wall, Which are the Fairest Theories of All?' *International Studies Quarterly* 33 (1989), 255–61.

19 For an early work guided by a similar conception, see S. Mendlovitz, ed., *On the Creation of a Just World Order: Preferred Worlds for the 1990s* (New York: Free Press, 1975).

20 R.J. Vincent, *Human Rights and International Relations* (Cambridge: Cambridge University Press, 1986), 124.

21 *Inside/Outside: International Relations as Political Theory* (Cambridge: Cambridge University Press, 1993), 90.

22 See Alan James, *Sovereign Statehood: The Basis of International Society* (London: Allen and Unwin, 1986), for an extended discussion of various facets of sovereignty, including the political, legal, jurisdictional, and moral 'quarrels' that have arisen.

23 Thus the condition of anarchy in the international system maintains this primitive state. Hobbes also writes: 'the bonds of words are too weak to bridle mens ambition, avarice, anger, and other Passions, without the fear of some coercive Power.' That power, the Leviathan, is not attainable in world politics as long as nation-states remain the primary units of organization. Therefore each must seek its own security. T. Hobbes, *Leviathan* (1651), C.B. MacPherson, ed. (New York: Penguin, 1968), 196.

24 *The Territorial Imperative: A Personal Inquiry into the Animal Origins of Property and Nations* (New York: Atheneum, 1966), 336. Ardrey continues that in war, 'a certain local anxiety may be generated, the anxiety of wives and mothers. But it is a small force as compared to the anxiety of losing the war itself.'

25 See John Herz, *International Politics in the Atomic Age* (New York: Columbia University Press, 1959).

26 Palme Commission on Disarmament and Security Issues, *A World at Peace: Common Security in the 21st Century* (Stockholm, 1989). For prescriptions for comprehensive security, see Robert Johansen, 'Toward Post-Nuclear Global Security: An Overview,' in Burns Weston, ed., *Alternative Security: Living without Nuclear Deterrence* (Boulder, CO: Westview, 1990), 220–60; and A. Westing, 'The Environmental Component of Comprehensive Security,' *Bulletin of Peace Proposals* 20 (1989), 129–34.

27 For an excellent discussion see Lothar Brock, 'Peace through Parks: The

Environment on the Peace Research Agenda,' *Journal of Peace Research* 28:4 (1991), 407–23.

28 Barry Buzan, 'New Patterns of Global Security in the Twenty-First Century,' *International Affairs* 67:3 (1991), 431–51; 433. See also his *People, States and Fear: An Agenda For International Security Studies in the Post-Cold War Era* (London: Harvester Wheatsheaf, 1991).

29 See, for example, Richard Ullman, 'Redefining Security,' *International Security*, 8:1 (1983), 129–53; and Theodore Sorensen, 'Rethinking National Security,' *Foreign Affairs* 69:3 (1990), 1–18. Sorensen, calling for a new 'national thesis,' reifies old notions of security: 'In a world that is still heavily armed, highly volatile, and increasingly complex, our instinctive obligations of national self-preservation and self-esteem require us to secure before all else the survival of our own nation's independence, institutions, and inhabitants' (p. 3).

30 Norman Myers, 'Environment and Security,' *Foreign Policy* 74 (Spring 1989), 23–41.

31 As does Nicholas Eberstadt, who writes of threats to Western security related to rising Southern, and declining Northern, populations. See 'Population Change and National Security,' *Foreign Affairs* 70:3 (1991), 115–31.

32 Janet Welsh Brown, ed., *In the U.S. Interest: Resources, Growth, and Security in the Developing World* (Boulder, CO: Westview, 1990).

33 Jessica Tuchman Mathews, 'Redefining Security,' *Foreign Affairs* 68:2 (1989), 175. This article contains a concise overview of contemporary global environmental problems.

34 Peter Gleick, 'Environment and Security: The Clear Connections,' *Bulletin of the Atomic Scientists* 47:3 (1991), 16–21.

35 Daniel Deudney, 'Environment and Security: Muddled Thinking,' *Bulletin of the Atomic Scientists*, April 1991, 22–8; 24 and 25.

36 Daniel Deudney, 'The Mirage of Eco-War: The Weak Relationship among Global Environmental Change, National Security and Interstate Violence.' In I. Rowlands and M. Greene, *Global Environmental Change and International Relations* (London: Macmillan, 1992), 169–91; 182. See also his 'Environment and Security: Muddled Thinking,' *Bulletin of the Atomic Scientists* April 1991, 22–8; and 'The Case against Linking Environmental Degradation and National Security,' *Millennium* 19:3 (1990), 461–76. For the best collection of related work, consult the ongoing reports of the Woodrow Wilson Center's Environmental Change and Security Project.

37 Richard Falk, *This Endangered Planet: Prospects and Proposals for Human Survival* (New York: Random House, 1971), 37–8.

38 David Newman, 'The New Diplomatic Agenda: Are Governments Ready?' *International Affairs* 65:1 (1989), 29–42; 35.

39 R.B.J. Walker, 'Security, Sovereignty, and the Challenge of World Politics,' *Alternatives* 15 (199?), 3–27; 10 and 12.

40 Lynn Miller writes: '*the best social order would permit very great local control and autonomy in policy making, but link us in a global network of social solidarity*' (emphasis in original). Miller, *Global Order*, 215.

41 We should be careful, however, of a blanket celebration of nonstate actors. First, we must include multinational corporations in this category, and many analysts are sceptical about the long-term transformative potential of a world organized according to the rules of economic efficiency and production. Second, all actors have their own interests and agendas, and many would impose a morality on others, which would lead to understandable charges of 'cultural imperialism.' I explore this idea at greater length in Chapter 5.

42 For a fascinating account of the spread of European power in ecological terms, see Alfred Crosby's *Ecological Imperialism: The Biological Expansion of Europe, 900–1900* (Cambridge: Cambridge University Press, 1986).

43 Timothy Shaw, 'Security Redefined: Unconventional Conflict in Africa,' in S. Wright and J. Brownfoot, eds., *Africa in World Politics: Changing Perspectives* (London: Macmillan, 1987), 17–34; 18.

44 Ken Booth, *Strategy and Ethnocentrism* (New York: Holmes and Meier, 1979), 145.

45 A. Wolfers, 'National Security as an Ambiguous Symbol,' *Political Science Quarterly* 67:4 (1952), 481–502; 482.

46 Rajni Kothari, 'Peace in an Age of Transformation,' in R.B.J. Walker, ed., *Culture, Ideology, and World Order* (Boulder, CO: Westview, 1984), 323–61; 327.

47 Dean Mann is not profoundly optimistic: on the subject of paradigm change he writes that 'the achievement of even a fraction of the objectives sought by environmental analysts within a reasonable time period would be an achievement of monumental proportions.' He is quite correct. 'Environmental Learning in a Decentralized Political World,' *Journal of International Affairs* 44:2 (1991), 301–38; 306. The 1997 Kyoto summit on global warming provides ample evidence of just how difficult moving ahead on such issues will be.

48 See J. Donnelly, 'International Human Rights after the Cold War,' in Klare and Thomas, ed., *World Security*, 236–54.

49 I.G. Simmons, *Changing the Face of the Earth: Culture, Environment, History* (Oxford: Basil Blackwell, 1989), 270.

50 E. Nelson, 'Britain's Aboriginal Sin,' *Bulletin of the Atomic Scientists* 48:6 (1992), 8–9.

51 Quoted in, L.S., Wiseberg, 'The Vienna World Conference on Human Rights,' in E. Fawcett and H. Newcombe, eds., *United Nations Reform: Looking Ahead after Fifty Years* (Toronto: Science for Peace/University of Toronto, 1995), 173–82; 177.

52 Lothar Brock, 'Peace through Parks'; 418.

53 Richard Ashley, *The Political Economy of War and Peace: The Sino-Soviet-American Triangle and the Modern Security Problematique* (New York: Nichols, 1980), 301 (original is in italics).

54 Vincent, *Human Rights*, 151.

55 Mel Gurtov, *Global Politics in the Human Interest* (Boulder, CO: Rienner, 1988), 18. Many studies that explicitly question the validity of the various norms associated with militarism from an ecological standpoint are of ecofeminist origin. Virginia Held, for example, believes that gender makes a significant difference, since men have traditionally been trained to think in patterns of abstraction, decontextualizing problems and seeking to dominate emotion with rationality. 'Such training provides both a moral and an emotional insulation that makes violence at any level more comfortable,' including violence against nature. 'Gender as an Influence on Cultural Norms Relating to War and the Environment,' in Westing, ed., *Cultural Norms, War and the Environment*, 44–52; 47. In the same volume see Birgit Brock-Utne, 'Formal Education as a Force in Shaping Cultural Norms Relating to War and the Environment,' 83–100; and Brian Easlea, *Fathering the Unthinkable: Masculinity, Scientists and the Nuclear Arms Race* (London: Pluto, 1983).

56 Ibid., 45.

57 John McMurtry, *Unequal Freedoms: The Global Market as an Ethical System* (Toronto: Garamond, 1998).

58 Gareth Porter and Janet Welsh Brown, *Global Environmental Politics* (Boulder, CO: Westview Press, 1991). See in particular 'International Security and the Environment,' 108–23.

59 *Human Security and Mutual Vulnerability: An Exploration into the Global Political Economy of Development and Underdevelopment* (Ottawa: International Development Research Centre, 1995).

60 'War and the Environment,' in J. Allen, ed., *Environment 1993/1994* (Guilford, Conn.: Annual Editions, 1993), 34–5.

Chapter 2.   State Violence: Genocide

1 An earlier version of this essay first appeared as 'This Age of Genocide: Conceptual and Institutional Implications,' *International Journal* 50:3 (1995), 594–618. I thank the editors of the journal for helpful comments.

2 A United Nations report by three African jurists concluded that the killings were part of a larger plan aimed at exterminating the Tutsis; they also noted that 'some reliable estimates put the number of victims at close to one million, but the world is unlikely ever to know the exact figure.' *Globe and Mail* (Toronto), 3 December 1994, A13.

3 See Alain Destexhe, 'The Third Genocide,' *Foreign Policy* 97 (Winter, 1994–5), 3–17; Milton Leitenberg, 'Rwanda, 1994: International Incompetence Produces Genocide,' *Peacekeeping and International Relations* 23 (1994), 6–10; and Holly Burkhalter, 'The Question of Genocide: The Clinton Administration and Rwanda,' *World Policy Journal* 11:4 (1994/5), 44–54. The neighbouring state of Burundi has an equally distressing political past, and may be on the verge of similar chaos; and civil war rages throughout the Central African region, in Angola, Sudan, Uganda, and Congo.

4 Raul Hilberg, *The Destruction of the European Jews* (New York: Holmes and Meier, 1983), see also Helen Fein, *Accounting for Genocide: National Response and Jewish Victimization during the Holocaust* (New York: Free Press, 1979).

5 Andrew Bell-Fialkoff, 'A Brief History of Ethnic Cleansing,' *Foreign Affairs* 72 (1993), 110–21.

6 See, for example, John Stackhouse, 'UN Report Warns of Threat to Children,' *Globe and Mail*, 15 December 1994, A9.

7 For two interesting discussions on sovereignty, see Alan James, *Sovereign Statehood: The Basis of International Society* (London: Allen and Unwin, 1986), and R.B.J. Walker, *Inside/Outside: International Relations as Political Theory* (New York: Cambridge University Press 1993).

8 Central News, press release DH1745, *UN Daily Highlights* (Internet), 6 October 1994.

9 Ethan Nadelmann, 'Global Prohibition Regimes: The Evolution of Norms in International Society,' *International Organization* 44 (Autumn 1990), 481–526; 481.

10 Milton Leitenberg, 'Anatomy of a Massacre,' *The New York Times*, 31 July 1994, 15.

11 See Hurst Hannum, *Autonomy, Sovereignty, and Self-Determination: The Accommodation of Conflicting Rights* (Philadelphia: University of Pennsylvania Press, 1990), 220.

12 See his landmark *Axis Rule in Occupied Europe* (Washington: Carnegie Endowment, 1944), 79.

13 In the 1970 U.S. Senate Foreign Relations Sub-Committee Hearings on the Genocide Convention and Its Aftermath report, the committee chair, Senator Frank Church, questioned if the convention wasn't 'really an effort to pound a few more nails into Hitler's coffin'; the Senate continued to reject

ratification, concerned with its implications for sovereignty and federalism, until 1986. Quoted in *Hearings Before a Subcommittee of the Committee on Foreign Relations, United States Senate, Ninety-First Congress, Second Session,* 1970, 61–2.

14 Nagendra Singh, 'The Development of International Law,' in Adam Roberts and Benedict Kingsbury, eds., *United Nations, Divided World: The UN's Roles in International Relations* (Oxford: Clarendon Press, 1993), 384–419; 394. The Draft Convention is UN doc. E/447 (1947).

15 This line, which referred essentially to German attempts at creating a 'master race' and forced sterilization, clearly qualifies the Serbian rape campaign in Bosnia as genocidal.

16 Article II, *Convention on the Prevention and Punishment of the Crime of Genocide,* adopted unanimously by the UN General Assembly, 9 December 1948; *UN Treaty Series,* Vol. 78, p. 277. Entered into force 12 January 1951.

17 Ibid., Article III.

18 For a concise description and evaluation of the convention, see Hans-Heinrich Jescheck, 'Genocide,' in Rudolf Bernhardt, director, *Encyclopedia of International Law, Volume Eight: Human Rights and the Individual in International Law* (Amsterdam: North-Holland, 1985), 255–7.

19 Destexhe, 'The Third Genocide,' 5.

20 *Accounting for Genocide,* 7.

21 Wulf Kansteiner, 'From Exception to Exemplum: The New Approach to Nazism and the "Final Solution,"' *History and Theory: Studies in the Philosophy of History* 33:2 (1994), 145–71; 147.

22 Ibid., 155. The most important contribution to this thinking was, arguably, Hannah Arendt's famous coverage of the Adolf Eichmann trial in Israel. See her *Eichmann in Jerusalem: A Report of the Banality of Evil* (New York: Viking, 1963). Eichmann was hung for crimes against humanity in 1962.

23 *Modernity and the Holocaust* (Ithaca, NY: Cornell University Press, 1989), 7.

24 *Globe and Mail,* 3 December 1994, A13.

25 Article 22 of the regulations annexed to The Hague Convention of 1907.

26 To quote two international legal experts: 'In light of the multifarious effects of hydrogen-bombs, and particularly the area of devastation from "fall-out" with its unpredictable genetic effects, it could not be said that a belligerent in resorting to thermo-nuclear weapons was adopting a means of injuring the enemy which was "limited" in any sense of the word.' Nagendra Singh and Edward McWhinney, *Nuclear Weapons and Contemporary International Law,* Second Edition (Dordrecht: Martinus Nijhoff, 1989), 115–16.

27 *Deterring Democracy* (New York: Hill and Wang, 1992), 127. Chomsky compares current American policies with the Opium War (1839–42).

28 Hiroshi Nakajima, quoted in Chomsky, *Deterring Democracy,* 241; for Shue, see his *Basic Rights: Subsistence, Affluence, and U.S. Foreign Policy* (Princeton: Princeton University Press, 1980).

29 *Verdict of the International Tribunal of Indigenous Peoples and Oppressed Nations in the USA* (San Francisco: American Indian Movement, 4 October 1992). Reported in the *Internet on the Holocaust and Genocide*, 44–6 (1993), 13–14.

30 Pierre van den Berghe, 'Introduction,' in same, ed., *State Violence and Ethnicity* (Niwot: University Press of Colorado, 1990), 1–18; 6.

31 Kuper, *Genocide* (New Haven: Yale University Press, 1981), 161. We should note, however, that Kuper assumes a minimalist definition of genocide in his work.

32 Destexhe, 'The Third Genocide,' 4.

33 Hannum, *Autonomy, Sovereignty, and Self-Determination*, 464.

34 Mark Zacher and Richard Matthew, 'Liberal International Theory: Common Threads, Divergent Strands,' in C. Kegley, ed., *Controversies in International Relations Theory*, 107–49; 118.

35 *The Anarchical Society*, 26.

36 A fascinating intellectual treatment is Tony Kushner's *The Holocaust and the Liberal Imagination: A Social and Cultural History* (Oxford: Blackwell, 1994).

37 Barbara Harff, *Genocide and Human Rights: International Legal and Political Issues*, Monograph Series in World Affairs, 20:3, Graduate School of International Studies, University of Denver, 1985, 68. See also her *Genocide and Human Rights: International Legal and Political Issues* (Denver: University of Denver Press, 1984).

38 See Theodor Meron, 'The Case for War Crimes Trials in Yugoslavia,' *Foreign Affairs* 72:3 (1993), 122–35.

39 For contrasting perspectives on intervention, see H. Scott Fairley, 'State Actors, Humanitarian Intervention and International Law: Reopening the Pandora's Box,' *Georgia Journal of International and Cooperative Law*, 10:1 (1980), 29–63; and Thomas Weiss and Larry Minear, 'Do International Ethics Matter? Humanitarian Politics and the Sudan,' *Ethics and International Affairs* 5 (1991), 197–214. More generally, see R.J. Vincent's older but challenging *Nonintervention and International Order* (Princeton: Princeton University Press, 1974).

40 The tribunal was set up at the Hague in 1994 pursuant to Security Council Resolution 827, 25 May 1993. In contrast, the Allied War Crimes Tribunal, held at Nuremberg (20 November 1945–1 October 1946), sentenced twelve

defendants to be hanged. See Robert Conot, *Justice at Nuremberg* (New York: Harper and Row, 1983).

41 Speech to the General Assembly, UN Doc. A/34/D.V.14 (1979). Amin's government (1971–9) has been termed 'one of the most capricious, terror-ridden, and inhumane ... to emerge in sub-Saharan Africa.' R. Jackson and C. Rosberg, *Personal Rule in Black Africa: Prince, Autocrat, Prophet, Tryrant* (Berkeley: University of California Press, 1982), 259. The fact that Amin lives in comfortable exile is surely a mockery of any conception of justice.

42 Zacher and Mathews, *op. cit.*, 122–3.

43 'Liability for War Crimes,' in Peter Rowe, ed., *The Gulf War 1990–91 in International and English Law* (London: Routledge, 1993), 241–60; 260.

44 *Genocide: State Power and Mass Murder* (New Brunswick, NJ: Transaction Books, 1976), 21.

Chapter 3. Environmental Degradation: Ecocide

1 Parts of this chapter are forthcoming in an essay to be published in the journal *Environment and Security.* I am grateful to Simon Dalby for helpful comments.

2 For an early usage see Barry Weisberg, ed., *Ecocide in Indochina: The Ecology of War* (San Francisco: Canfield Press, 1970), and Richard Falk, 'Environmental Warfare and Ecocide,' *Bulletin of Peace Proposals* 4 (1973), 1–17.

3 For a detailed analysis see Adam Roberts, 'Failures in Protecting the Environment in the 1990–91 Gulf War,' in P. Rowe, ed., *The Gulf War 1990–91 in International and English Law*, London: Routledge and Sweet & Maxwell, 1993), 111–54; and Katherine Kelly, 'Declaring War on the Environment: The Failure of International Environmental Treaties during the Persian Gulf War,' *The American University Journal of International Law and Policy* 7:4 (1992), 921–50.

4 Mike Davis, 'The Dead West: Ecocide in Marlboro Country,' *New Left Review* 200 (July/August, 1993), 49–74.

5 This is Murray Feshbach and Alfred Friendly's *Ecocide in the USSR: Health and Nature under Siege* (New York: Basic Books, 1992).

6 Carl Sagan, 'Nuclear War and Climatic Catastrophe: Some Policy Implications,' *Foreign Affairs* 62 (Winter, 1982/84), 257–92; Jonathan Schell, *The Fate of the Earth* (New York: Knopf, 1982). For related, if more technical, material see R.P. Turco et al., 'Nuclear Winter: Global Consequences of Multiple Nuclear Explosions,' *Science* 23 December 1983, 1283–92; P. Ehrlich et al., 'Long-term Biological Consequences of Nuclear War,' Ibid., 1293–96; Jeannie Peterson,

ed., *The Aftermath: The Human and Ecological Consequences of Nuclear War* (New York: Pantheon, 1983).

7 T. Rueter and T. Kalil, 'Nuclear Strategy and Nuclear Winter,' *World Politics* 43 (July 1991), 587–607; 590. See also Brian Haig, 'Why We Must Accept Nuclear Winter Theory,' *Bulletin of Peace Proposals* 20:1 (1989), 81–8.

8 We might note that there are conflicting assessments of the ecological damage suffered by the Persian Gulf region, in particular by the deliberate lighting of oil fires and the dumping of oil into the Persian Gulf itself. One survey of oil contamination concluded that 'even the most heavily contaminated soils were judged relatively clean, roughly equal to samples from Buzzard's Bay near New York City,' which may say more about industrial pollution in general than Kuwait in particular. *Globe and Mail*, 20 August 1992; A8. As for the spectacular fires, in May 1991 the World Meteorological Organization estimated that more than 40,000 tonnes of sulfur dioxide, 3,000 tonnes of nitrous oxide, and 500,000 tonnes of carbon dioxide, and various other pollutants, were being emitted every day. See Paul Fauteux, 'The Use of the Environment as an Instrument of War in Occupied Kuwait,' in Bruno Schiefer, ed., *Verifying Obligations Respecting Arms Control and the Environment: A Post Gulf War Assessment* (Saskatoon: University of Saskatchewan, 1992), 35–79; and Elmer-Dewitt, 'A Man-Made Hell on Earth,' *Time*, 18 March 1991, 23.

9 For early examples of such work that do not attempt to hide an antiwar bias, see Jonathan Schell, *The Military Half: An Account of Destruction in Quang Ngai and Quang Tin* (New York: Knopf, 1968); Barry Weisberg, ed., *Ecocide in Indochina* ; and J. Neilands et al., *Harvest of Death: Chemical Warfare in Vietnam and Cambodia* (New York: Free Press, 1972).

10 From the introduction in Weisberg, *Ecocide in Indochina*, 4.

11 Environmental warfare involves manipulating the environment for hostile purposes; we will examine this in greater detail below. For an exploration of this term see Frank Barnaby, 'Environmental Warfare,' *Bulletin of the Atomic Scientists* 32 (1976), 36–43; Arthur Westing, 'Environmental Warfare,' *Environmental Law: Northwestern School of Lewis and Clark College* 15:4 (1985), 645–66; and Paul G. Lauren, 'War, Peace, and the Environment,' in R. Barrett, ed., *International Dimensions of the Environmental Crisis* (Boulder, CO: Westview, 1982), 75–92. In this context, for environmental warfare to constitute ecocide, one supposes, it must be highly successful.

12 E.F. Roots, 'International Agreements to Prohibit or Control Modification of the Environment for Military Purposes: An Historical Overview and Comments on Current Issues,' in Bruno Schiefer, ed., *Verifying Obligations Respecting Arms Control*, 13–34; 13.

13 See, for example, *Warfare in a Fragile World: Military Impact on the Human Environment* (London: Taylor and Francis, 1980); 'The Environmental Impact of Conventional Warfare,' in W. Barnaby, ed., *War and Environment* (Stockholm: Royal Ministry of Agriculture, 1981), 58–72; and 'The Environmental Component of Comprehensive Security,' *Bulletin of Peace Proposals* 20 (1989), 129–34; and, as editor, *Environmental Warfare: A Technical, Legal and Policy Appraisal* (London: Taylor and Francis, 1984); *Explosive Remnants of War: Mitigating the Environmental Effects* (Philadelphia: Taylor and Francis, 1985); *Global Resources and International Conflict: Environmental Factors in Strategic Policy and Action* (Oxford: Oxford University Press, 1986); *Cultural Norms, War and the Environment* (Oxford: Oxford University Press, 1988); and *Comprehensive Security for the Baltic: An Environmental Approach* (London: Sage, 1989).

14 A. Westing, *Warfare in a Fragile World*, 14–19.

15 J.P. Robinson, 'The Effects of Weapons on Ecosystems,' *United Nations Environment Program Studies, Volume One* (Toronto: Permagon, 1979), 15; see also A. Westing, ed., *Herbicides in War* (London: Taylor and Francis, 1984). For a fascinating legal and sociological discussion of the reactions of American Vietnam veterans to Agent Orange, see J. Jacobs and D. McNamara, 'Vietnam Veterans and the Agent Orange Controversy,' *Armed Forces and Society* 13:1 (1986), 57–80.

16 Richard Falk wrote in 1973: 'Surely it is no exaggeration to consider the forests and plantations treated by Agent Orange as an Auschwitz for environmental values, certainly not from the perspective of such a distinct environmental species as the mangrove tree or nipa palm.' 'Environmental Warfare and Ecocide: Facts, Appraisal, and Proposals,' *Bulletin of Peace Proposals* 4:1 (1973), 84.

17 Ibid., 44; also, *Report of the Special Mission on International Assistance for the Reconstruction of Viet Nam*, appointed by the secretary general in accordance with General Assembly Resolution 32/3 (UN Doc. 78–02689). Robinson, discussing this 'biocide,' notes that the effects of forest destruction extend far beyond the forested area itself. We might note that U.S. President Gerald Ford renounced the first use of herbicides – except for control of vegetation within U.S. bases and installations or around immediate defence parameters – in 1975. *Department of State Bulletin*, 5 May 1975, 576–7. See also J. Lewallen, *Ecology of Destruction: Indochina* (Baltimore: Penguin, 1971); R. Stevens, *The Trail: A History of the Ho Chi Minh Trail and the Role of Nature in the War in Viet Nam* (New York: Garland, 1993); and R. and J. Wolkomir, 'Caught in the Crossfire,' *International Wildlife*, January–February 1992, 4–11.

18 Robert Harris and Jeremy Paxman, *A Higher Form of Killing: The Secret Story of Gas and Germ Warfare* (London: Chatto and Windus, 1982), 27.

19 Senate Foreign Relations Committee, Subcommittee on Oceans and International Environment, 'Weather Modification,' 93rd Congress, 2nd Session, 87–123; Seymour Hersch, 'Rainmaking Is Used as Weapon by U.S.,' *New York Times*, 3 July 1972. It became clear, 'in a macabre way,' writes Georg Breuer, that cloud seeding had occurred in Vietnam, Laos, and Cambodia when 'the Weather Engineering Corporation [WEC] of Canada and their affiliates in the USA accused the American government of having used a special cartridge developed by their firm for seeding operations in Southeast Asia, thereby infringing the patent law, and [WEC] demanded payment of $95 million in licence fees.' Georg Breuer, *Weather Modification: Prospects and Problems*, trans. Hans Morth (Cambridge: Cambridge University Press, 1979), 71–2.

20 L. Juda, 'Negotiating a Treaty on Environmental Modification Warfare: The Convention on Environmental Warfare and Its Impact upon Arms Control Negotiations,' *International Organization* 32:4 (1978), 975–92; 976, n3. Juda is referring to a claim made by a former Department of Defense consultant, Lowell Ponte, in the *International Herald Tribune*, 29 June 1976, p. 2.

21 G. MacDonald, 'Geophysical Warfare: How to Wreck the Environment,' in N. Calder, ed., *Unless Peace Comes* (London: Allen Lane, 1968), 165–84; 170; and Breuer, *Weather Modification*, 71.

22 Quoted in Breuer, *Weather Modification*, 73.

23 For examples of the environmental effect of warfare, see Gregory Wirick, 'Environment and Security: The Case of Central America,' *Peace and Security* (Canadian Centre for International Peace and Security), Summer 1989, 2–3; Robert Rice, 'A Casualty of War: The Nicaraguan Environment,' *Technology Review* 92:4 (1989), 62–71; and the many articles in Michael Cranna, ed., *The True Cost of Conflict* (London: Earthscan, 1994).

24 Ian Robinson, 'The East Timor Conflict (1975–),' in Cranna, ed., *The True Cost*, 1–24, 10–11.

25 Angela Burke and Gordon Macdonald, 'The Former Yugoslavia Conflict (1991–),' in Cranna, *The True Cost*, 155–96; 176. See also 'Cries of "Ecocide" from Croatia,' *Earth Island Journal* 7:1 (1992), 17.

26 Zeremariam Fre, 'The Legacy of War,' in O. Bennett, ed., *Greenwar: Environment and Conflict* (London: Panos Institute, 1991), 131–42; 134. See also A. Westing, ed., 'Disarmament, Environment, and Development and Their Relevance to the Least Developed Countries,' *UN Institute for Disarmament Research Paper No. 10* (Geneva: UNIDR and UNEP, 1991).

27 See David Russell, 'The Kuwait Oil Fires and Their Environmental Effects,'

in Bruno Schiefer, ed., *Verifying Obligations Respecting Arms Control and the Environment: A Post Gulf War Assessment* (Saskatoon: University of Saskatchewan, 1992), 85–96; 88. Also, T.Y. Canby, 'After the Storm,' *National Geographic* 181:2 (1991), 2–35.

28 This has occurred southwest of the Tigris. According to one report, 7,500 out of 20,000 km² of marsh has been destroyed. Gregory Quinn, 'The Iraq Conflict (1990–), in Cranna, *The True Cost*, 25–54; 33.

29 But see Roberts, 'Failures in Portecting the Environment,' which argues that more could have been done in this regard. See also L.C. Green, *The Contemporary Law of Armed Conflict* (Manchester: Manchester University Press, 1993), 131–2 and 289–90.

30 Arthur Westing, 'The Military Sector *vis-à-vis* the Environment,' *Journal of Peace Research* 25:2 (1988), 257–64.

31 Johan Galtung, *Environment, Development, and Military Activity: Towards Alternative Security Doctrines* (Oslo: Universitetsforlaget, 1982). We should note that the present author insists, with others such as Martin Shaw, that war preparation 'includes all forms of organization capable of producing war, irrespective of whether there is any intention or desire to use them.' M. Shaw, *Post-Military Society: Militarism, Demilitarization and War at the End of the Twentieth Century* (Cambridge: Polity, 1991), 11.

32 See D. Hilderley, 'Cleanup of Radar Bases May Cost $250-million, Official Says,' *Globe and Mail*, 23 April 1993, A5.

33 Seth Shulman, *The Threat at Home: Confronting the Toxic Legacy of the U.S. Military* (Boston: Beacon, 1992). On the effects of nuclear production by the U.S. military, see U.S. Office of Technology Report, 'Complex Cleanup: The Environmental Legacy of Nuclear Weapons Production' (Washington: USGPO, 1991). More generally see Anne McIlroy, 'Armed Forces Are World's Biggest Polluters, Report Says,' *Kingston Whig-Standard* 18 March 1992.

34 Robert Alvarez and Arjun Makhijani, 'Hidden Legacy of the Arms Race: Radioactive Waste,' *Technology Review* 91:6 (1988), 42–51. At the Savannah River plant, experts had predicted that plutonium waste would not reach the water table for 1 million years: it took only 20. Ibid., 47. See also John Ahearne, 'Fixing the Nation's Nuclear Weapons Plants,' *Technology Review* 92:5 (1989), 24–9; and Stephen Hilgartner et al., 'Hanford: The Interim Reality,' in their *Nukespeak: The Selling of Nuclear Technology in America* (New York: Penguin, 198), 150–9.

35 'Deadly Nuclear Waste Seems to Have Leaked in Washington State,' *New York Times*, 28 February 1993, 31. Long-term clean-up plans include pumping toxic sledge to a special factory where it will be mixed with molten

glass and stuffed into logs of steel. Other significant problems elsewhere, according to Steele, are as follows:

SAVANNAH RIVER: 192,000 acres; 10 of 51 large steel tanks containing high-level waste are leaking. Tuscaloosa Aquifer contaminated. An accident in December 1991 leaked tritium into the Savannah River, further straining relations between DOE and members of the local community.

IDAHO: 570,000 acres; has 61 per cent of U.S. transuranic wastes stored in 55-gallon drums; plutonium detected in a clay layer about 110 feet below the site; hazardous chemicals found in groundwater at about 600 feet, namely carbon tetrachloride and trichloroethylene and radiation.

FERNALD: 128 acres; contaminated groundwater is migrating off-site toward an important source of drinking water, the Great Miami Aquifer.

36 Jeffrey Walker, 'A Green Peace: The Closure of Overseas Military Installations and the Environmental Liability of the U.S. Government,' *Georgetown International Environmental Law Review* 3:2 (1990), 437–56.

37 T. Ivanova and N. Glovatskaia, 'Criteria and Principles of Developing an Ecological Policy,' trans. A. Schultz, *The Soviet Review* 33:1 (1992), 32–44. Indeed, in the saddest of commercial ironies, cleaning up the Soviet Union has been a source of potential employment for American firms. It was announced in London on 31 January 1992 and reported in the *Financial Times* that 'the International Disarmament Corporation, a company that will specialize in the dismantling of Soviet nuclear weapons systems, has been formed by Lockhead, Olin, and the McDermott International subsidiary Babcock and Wilcox ... the group will offer its service to the four commonwealth states that lack the [appropriate] expertise.'

38 'Nuclear Plant Dosed 450,000 in Accidents,' *Globe and Mail*, 28 January 1993.

39 Peter Gizewski (Canadian Centre for Global Security), 'Military Activity and Environmental Security: The Case of the Arctic,' paper presented to 'Environmental Security After Communism' conference, Carleton University, Ottawa, 26–27 February 1993. Much of the information presented here was initially gathered by Gizewski.

40 Wheeler adds: 'Our entire social order faces an ecosystem "depression" that will make 1929 look like a shower at a garden party.' 'Introduction' in C. Fadiman and J. White, eds., *Ecocide ... And Thoughts toward Survival* (New York: James Feel and Associates, in collaboration with the Center for the Study of Democratic Institutions, 1971).

41 See, for example, Daniel Faber, *Environment under Fire: Imperialism and the Ecological Crisis in Central America* (New York: Monthly Review, 1993).

42 Feshbach and Friendly, *Ecocide in the USSR*, 49.

43 Of course, there are many links between natural disasters and the inade-

quacy of human response, especially in terms of certain segments of a population suffering greater ill effects. See Terry Cannon, 'Vulnerability Analysis and the Explanation of "Natural" Disasters,' in A. Varley, ed., *Disasters, Development and Environment* (New York: John Wiley, 1994), 13–30.

44 Maria Mies and Vandana Shiva, *Ecofeminism* (Halifax: Fernwood Publications, 1993), 2.

45 For example, V.G. Venturini uses the term – though he does not define it – in *Partners in Ecocide: Australia's Complicity in the Uranium Cartel* (Clifton Hill: Rigmarole, 1982).

46 None of this is to deny the exceptional importance of the increase in species extinction. See Les Kaufman and Kenneth Mallory, eds., *The Last Extinction*, Second Edition (Cambridge, MA: MIT Press, 1993).

47 I make no attempt to replicate here the wealth of printed material on environmental regimes or on critics of global managerialism. See for example, L. Caldwell, *International Environmental Policy: Emergence and Dimensions* (Durham, NC: Duke University Press, 1996); P. Haas, R. Keohane, and M. Levy, eds., *Institutions for the Earth: Sources of Effective International Environmental Protection* (Cambridge: MIT Press, 1993); and W. Sachs, ed., *Global Ecology: The New Arena of Political Conflict* (London: Zed, 1993).

48 See Eric Laferrière and Peter Stoett, *International Relations Theory and Ecological Thought: Towards a Synthesis* (London: Routledge, 1999).

49 Thomas Homer-Dixon, Jeffrey Boutwell, and George Rathjens, 'Environmental Scarcity and Violent Conflict,' forthcoming. The most cogent published explication of this thesis is written by Thomas Homer-Dixon, whose article is required reading for anyone interested in this issue. 'On the Threshold: Environmental Changes and Causes of Acute Conflict,' *International Security* 16:2 (1991), 76–116.

50 Olivia Bennett, ed., *Greenwar*.

51 Reiduff K. Molvaer, 'Environmentally Induced Conflicts? A Discussion Based on Studies from the Horn of Africa,' *Bulletin of Peace Proposals* 22:2 (1991), 175–88.

52 Fritz Visser, 'Recent Developments in the Joint Management of International Non-Maritime Water Resources in Africa,' *The Comparative and International Law Journal of Southern Africa* 22:1 (1989), 59–92.

53 Daniel Deudney, 'The Mirage of Eco-War: The Weak Relationship among Global Environmental Change, National Security and Interstate Violence,' in I. Rowlands and M. Greene, *Global Environmental Change and International Relations* (London: Macmillan, 1992), 169–91; 183. It should be noted that this point is used by Deudney for specific purposes, discussed below.

54 Joyce Starr, *U.S. Foreign Policy on Water Resources in the Middle East* (Washington: Center For Strategic and International Studies, 1987).
55 Joyce Starr, 'Water Wars,' *Foreign Policy* 82 (Spring, 1991), 17–36; 19. The Middle Eastern situation is complicated by unsettled political problems. For example, the West Bank aquifer supplies 25 to 40 per cent of Israeli's water. One student of international river basins recently concluded that 'cooperative agreements result only when denial of access to the waters threatens national security, and when such arrangements are advocated or imposed by a hegemon.' M. Lowi, *The Politics of Water under Conditions of Scarcity and Conflict: The Jordan River and Riparian States*, PhD dissertation, Princeton, 1990. See also Peter Gleick, 'Climate Changes, International Rivers, and International Security; The Nile and the Colorado,' in T. Minger, ed., *Greenhouse Glasnost: The Crisis of Global Warming* (New York: Ecco, 1990), 147–65; and M. Falkenmark, 'Fresh Waters as a Factor in Strategic Policy and Action,' in A. Westing, ed., *Global Resources and International Conflict*, 85–113.
56 We are cautioned, however, before attributing too much causal significance to environmental degradation. For example, two analysts conclude that in the Rwandan case, although the violence 'occurred in conditions of severe environmental scarcity, because the Arusha Accords and regime insecurity were the key factors motivating the Hutu elite, environmental scarcity played a much more peripheral role.' V. Percival and T. Homer-Dixon, *Environmental Scarcity and Violent Conflict: The Case of Rwanda* (American Association for the Advancement of Science and the University of Toronto, Project on Environment, Population, and Security, 1995), 15.
57 Kevin McMahon, 'Arctic Ecocide,' *Peace Magazine* (Toronto), 5:3 (June 1989), 16–17.
58 Principle 24 of the Rio Declaration of June 1992 offered what Adam Roberts calls an 'anodyne formula': 'Warfare is inherently destructive of sustainable development. States shall therefore respect international law providing protection for the environment in times of armed conflict and co-operate in its further development, as necessary.' Adams demands a clearer method than exists presently to establish the idea that 'wanton destruction of the environment is a serious war crime,' but makes it clear that he is not implying that 'war can ever be brought completely within a strict legal framework, or that the world can be made safe for clean wars.' 'Failures in Protecting the Environment,' 146.
59 For useful surveys see Lynton Keith Caldwell's authoritative *International Environmental Policy: From the Twentieth to the Twenty-First Century*, Third Edition (Durham, NC: Duke University Press, 1996); Peter Haas, 'Evolving

International Environmental Law: Changing Practices of National Sovereignty,' in N. Choucri, ed., *Global Accord: Environmental Challenges and International Responses* (Cambridge: MIT Press, 1993), 401–28; and Peter Sands, 'Enforcing Environmental Security: The Challenges of Compliance with International Obligations, *Journal of International Affairs* 46:2, 367–90.

60 See Edith Brown Weiss, 'Intergenerational Equity: Toward an International Legal Framework,' in N. Choucri, ed., *Global Accord: Environmental Challenges and International Responses* (Cambridge: MIT Press, 1993), 333–53; D. Freestone, 'The Precautionary Principle.' in R. Churchill and D. Freestone, ed., *International Law and Global Climate Change* (London: Graham and Trotham, 1991), 21–39; and S.M. Garcia, 'The Precautionary Principle: Its Implications in Captive Fisheries Management,' *Ocean and Coastal Management* 22, 99–125.

61 'Environmental Ethics and Global Governance: Engaging the International Liberal Tradition,' *Global Governance* 3, 213–31; 218.

62 I.G. Simmons, *Changing the Face of the Earth: Culture, Environment, History* (Oxford: Basil Blackwell, 1989), 315.

Chapter 4.   Population Displacement: Refugees

1 Another version of this chapter, which focused on the Canadian foreign policy context, appeared as 'Redefining "Environmental Refugees"': Canada and the UNHCR,' in *Canadian Foreign Policy* 2:3 (1995), 29–42.

2 For a short article that stresses the relationship between predictions of global warming and predictions of related population displacement, see Norman Myers, 'Environmental Refugees in a Globally Warmed World: Estimating the Scope of What Could Well Become a Prominent International Phenomenon,' *Bioscience*, 43:11 (1993), 752–61.

3 The most widely publicized predictions of potential shoreline erosion and coastal flooding appeared with the Intergovernmental Panel on Climate Change's *Climate Change: The IPCC Scientific Assessment*, Final Report of Working Group 1 (New York: Cambridge University Press, 1990).

4 For example: 'Rainfall in the Sahel depends upon the reach of the Inter-Tropical Convergence Zone (ITCZ), the equatorial rendezvous for tropical air masses. In the summer months, warm maritime air condenses into monsoon clouds; how far north the clouds reach depends on the relative strength of atmospheric circulations over the oceans which in turn may be affected by small differences in sea temperatures between the North and South Atlantic. If the ITCZ contracts a fraction, the consequence for Sahelian farmers at the edge of the rainfall belt is certain crop failure.' Nigel

Cross, *The Sahel: The People's Right to Development* (London: Minority Rights Group, 1990), 16; see also T. Downing, 'Vulnerability to Hunger in Africa: A Climate Change Perspective,' *Global Environmental Change*, 1:5 (1991), 365–80.

5 Volker Turk, 'Refugees in the Third World: An Examination in the International Refugee Law Context,' in the *Association for the Study of the World Refugee Problem Bulletin (Vierteljahresschrift fur Fluchtlingsfragen)* 29:1 (1991), 12–16.

6 Or, as Angier Biddle Duke, former U.S. Ambassador to Cambodia, once said: 'We have ... thrown life-belts to the drowning, but left them in the sea.' Quoted in Judy Magotte, *Disposable People? The Plight of Refugees* (New York: Orbis, 1992), 35. This metaphor seems especially apt, given the related discussion on 'lifeboat ethics' introduced by biologist Garrett Hardin in the 1970s.

7 Essam El-Hinnawi, *Environmental Refugees* (Nairobi: UNEP, 1985), 4. See in particular Werner Fornos, 'Desperate Departures: The Flight of Environmental Refugees,' in *Toward the 21st Century* (The Population Institute), No. 4, 1992, a report presented at the UN Expert Group Meeting on Population, Distribution and Migration, 18–22 January 1993, in Santa Cruz, Bolivia (in preparation for the 1994 International Conference on Population); and Jodi Jacobson, *Environmental Refugees: A Yardstick of Habitability* (Washington: Worldwatch Institute, 1988). Finally, for a broader treatment, see B. Kavanagh and S. Lonergan, *Environmental Degradation, Population Displacement and Global Security: An Overview of the Issues* (Ottawa: Canadian Global Change Program Incidental Report Series, Report IR92–1, 1992).

8 G.A. res. 36/148 – Report UN doc. A/41/324, 13 May 1986. Earlier, in 1984, the UNHCR convened a colloquium that met in Cartagena to discuss the Latin American refugee situation. The Cartagena Declaration recommended that *inter alia* the regional definition of a refugee should include persons who have fled their country 'because their lives, safety or freedom have been threatened by generalized violence, foreign aggression, internal conflicts, *massive violations of human rights or other circumstances which have seriously disturbed public order'* (italics added).

9 J. McGregor, *op. cit.* In a related regional development, Thailand's Royal Forestry Department (RFD) and the Royal Thai Army are planning to evict or redistribute the land holdings of over ten million people from national forest reserves, so that Thai and foreign corporations can lease land for fast-growing plantations of eucalyptus trees. One million people live inside the area planned for reforestation. Also, 250,000 families presently living in 2,500 village communities will be relocated to 5,290 square kilometres.

Dave Hubbel and Noel Rajesh, 'Not Seeing the People for the Forest: Thailand's Program of Reforestation by Forced Eviction,' *Refuge* 12:1 (1992), 20–1.

10 Arthur Westing, 'Environmental Refugees: A Growing Category of Displaced Persons,' *Environmental Conservation* 19:3 (1992), 201–8. Westing estimates that roughly 0.8 percent of the world's people are recognized or unrecognized refugees. Recognized refugees fall under the official mandate of the UNHCR, which means they are fleeing political persecution, according to the *United Nations Convention Relating to the Status of Refugees*, adopted 28 July 1951 by the UN Conference of Plenipotentiaries on the Status of Refugees and Stateless Persons. Over 100 nations have signed the Convention, though some key Asian states are missing. There is also a broader definition endorsed by the Organization for African Unity (OAU).

11 Jon Martin Trolldalen et al., *Environmental Refugees – A Discussion Paper* (Oslo: World Foundation for Environment and Development and the Norwegian Refugee Council, 1992).

12 Paul Lewis, 'U.N. Hopes Number of Refugees Falls,' *New York Times*, 20 March 1994, 11.

13 Linda Hossie, 'Migration Increases as Search for Good Life Grows,' *Globe and Mail*, 22 June 1993.

14 One might, however, question some of these predictions. Alan Lipietz, for example, has estimated that 'ten billion people [!] over the next forty years will have to migrate to cope with climatic changes, in the context of a finite world with increased racial tension.' Though the context sounds entirely plausible, the figure seems a little high at this point. *Towards a New Economic Order: Postfordism, Ecology and Democracy*, translated by Malcom Slater (Oxford: Polity, 1992), 172. See Myers, 'Environmental Refugees, for more conservative (though hardly less alarming) figures.

15 Edward Buehrig, *The United Nations and the Palestinian Refugees: A Study in Nonterritorial Administration* (Bloomington: Indiana University Press, 1971), 3.

16 See Kavanagh and Lonergan, *Environmental Degradation*, 4–5. They cite as an interesting example of a structuralist approach Mel Gurtov's 'global humanism,' to which we will return later in this chapter. See in particular his 'Open Borders: A Global-Humanist Approach to the Refugee Crisis,' *World Development* 19:5 (1991), 485–96; and, more generally, *Global Politics in the Human Interest* (Boulder, CO: Rienner, 1988).

17 See Thomas Homer-Dixon, 'On the Threshold: Environmental Changes and Causes of Acute Conflict,' *International Security* 16:2 (1991), 76–116; Olivia Bennett, ed., *Greenwar* (London: Pangos Institute, 1992); Reiduff K. Molvaer,

'Environmentally Induced Conflicts? A Discussion Based on Studies from the Horn of Africa,' *Bulletin of Peace Proposals*, 22:2 (1991), 175–88; and Jon Martin Trolldalen, 'Secondary Effects of Degradation: Environmental Refugees,' in his *International Environmental Conflicts Resolution: The Role of the UN* (Washington: World Foundation for Environment and Development, 1992), 155–71.

18 A. Dejene and J. Olivares, 'Integrating Environmental Issues into a Strategy for Sustainable Agricultural Development,' *World Bank Technical Paper No. 146* (Washington, 1991), 11.

19 R.P. Shaw, 'The Impact of Population Growth on Environment: The Debate Heats Up,' *Environmental Impact Assessment Review* 12:44 (1992), 11–36. See also Alan Simmance, 'The Impact of Large-Scale Refugee Movements and the Role of the UNHCR,' in John Rogge, ed., *Refugees: A Third World Dilemma* (New Jersey: Rowman and Littlefield, 1987), 9–14.

20 Harto Hakovirta, 'The Global Refugee Problem: A Model and Its Application,' *International Political Science Review* 14:1 (1993), 35–57; see page 39 for a graphic summary.

21 See A. Walker and P. Parmar, *Warrior Marks: Female Genital Mutilation and the Sexual Blinding of Women* (New York: Harcourt Brace, 1993).

22 For a concise treatment of the UNHCR within the formal UN system, see Leon Gordenker, 'The United Nations and Refugees,' in Lawrence Finkelstein, ed., *Politics in the United Nations System* (Durham: Duke University Press, 1988), 274–302.

23 See Hakovirto, 'The Global Refugee Problem,' and S. Blay and B. Tsameny, 'Reservations and Declarations under the 1951 Convention and the 1967 Protocol Relating to the Status of Refugees,' *International Journal of Refugee Law* 2:4 (1990), 527–61.

24 *Resolutions and Decisions of the General Assembly: 47th Session.*, Volume 1, Supplement 49 (A/47/49), 15 September–23 December 1992, 186–214; 187.

25 The current holder of this new position is Kazuo Watanabe of the Program Policy unit, Division of programs and Operational Support, UNHCR, Geneva. Personal correspondence, June 1993.

26 Personal correspondence with Qaz Shaukat Fareed, Director, Department of Humanitarian Affairs, United Nations, New York, September 1993.

27 Personal correspondence, summer of 1993. Puchala is the Director of the Institute of International Studies at the University of South Carolina.

28 V. Percival and T. Homer-Dixon, *Environmental Scarcity and Violent Conflict: The Case of Rwanda* (American Association for the Advancement of Science and the University of Toronto, Project on Environment, Population, and

Security, 1995), 4. The present author has spoken to eyewitnesses of this development, which is clearly unbearable from a humanitarian standpoint but which, in the absence of strong international pressure on the militias, will continue as long as there are camps.

29 Personal correspondence, September 1993, with Roger Winter, Director, U.S. Committee for Refugees.

30 The case of the Haitian refugees should have embarrassed the once liberal-minded Clinton Administration but seems to have been defused as an issue. The earlier policy of rejection continues. This raises another difficult conceptual element of refugee status questions: should related immigration be based on individual screening or on group identification? With regard to mass displacement, it is quite clear that we would have to assume the latter.

31 Personal correspondence, September 1993, with Qazi Shaukat Fareed, Director of the Department of Humanitarian Affairs, UN, New York.

32 Personal correspondence with Thomas Barned, now the Coordinator for Operations, International Catholic Migration Commission, Geneva, Switzerland, July 1993. The most infamous case of internal displacement is the recent 'safe haven' program in Bosnia.

33 Rosemary Rogers, 'The Future of Refugee Flows and Policies,' *International Migration Review* 36:4 (1992), 112–43.

34 As suggested in personal correspondence, June 1993, by Craig Murphy, professor of Political Science, Wellesley College. 'The problem with the UNHCR has to do with a decision to pursue a "voluntarist" solution to refugee problems when the Commission was established. For a variety of reasons, primarily the experience of the UNRRA and UNRWA, the U.S. did not want to create an international social service agency. Today, when all governments realize that the "refugee problem" will not simply "go away" some day, but probably just get larger and larger, the economic fears that pushed the U.S. to veto a more comprehensive UNHCR in the early 1950s are now shared by many more governments.'

35 Guy Goodwin-Gill, quoted in the January 1992 (#88) issue of the UNHCR's *Refugees*, 40. On the point of national interest, consider the following excerpt from a recent article in *The New York Times*: 'With the agency dependent on Western governments for more than 90 percent of its funding, Mrs. Ogata has been obliged to play down its traditional concern with resettling refugees in new countries of asylum and agree to care for them in camps until it is safe for them to return. This has aroused concern among outside experts and private charitable groups that the agency is accepting the political priorities of the major donor countries at the expense of upholding the

right to asylum, which its charter requires it to offer refugees. Mrs. Ogata says she is only being realistic.' Paul Lewis, 'U.N. Hopes Number of Refugees Falls,' 20 March 1994, 11.

36 Jo Ann McGregor, 'Refugees and the Environment,' in R. Black and V. Robinson, eds., *Geography and Refugees: Patterns and Processes of Change* (London: Belhaven, 1993), 157–70; 158.

37 David Keen, *Refugees: Rationing the Right to Life* (London: A Refugee Studies Programme Book, Zed, 1992), 75.

38 Even in the case of Haiti, it is clear that the fundamental social inequity that characterizes that state is off limits to interventionism; instead, the police force is being 'retrained' as a structural adjustment program is being implemented.

39 The quote is from personal correspondence with Douglas Ross, professor of Political Science at Simon Fraser University, September 1993. He feels that the increase in environmental refugees and economic migrants will continue to induce a 'swing right in European and North American politics towards the exclusionary siege mentality.'

40 Sir John Hope Simpson, *Refugees: Preliminary Report of a Survey* (London: Royal Institute of International Affairs, 1938), 193.

41 For a treatment of this perspective by the present author, see 'Human Rights and Environmental Security: Globalist Thinking in Canadian Foreign Policy,' *Policy Options Politiques* (Montreal, Canada), June 1994.

42 Gurtov, 'Open Borders,' 1991.

43 'Open and Closed Borders: Is the New World Order Creating a System of Global Apartheid?' *Refuge* 13:1 (1993), 6–10. For a short discussion on the 'decision logic of receiving states' from a 'national security interest' perspective, see Glenn Hastedt and Kay Knickrehm, 'Predicting State Response to Refugees,' in same, eds., *Toward the Twenty-First Century: A Reader in World Politics* (Englewood Cliffs, NJ: Prentice Hall, 1994), 382–9.

44 On the theory of functionalism in international politics, which retains relevance in this day and age of the stressed nation-state, see David Mitrany, *The Functional Theory of World Politics* (London: London School of Economics and Political Science, 1975). In his early academic career, during the Second World War, Mitrany studied the idea of coerced population transfers of minorities. He rejected the idea as not only inhumane but also misdirected. It would lead to a '*continuous* policy of [international] segregation ... the "New World" would be inaugurated by the suppression of an old freedom.' See Mitrany and Allen Fisher, 'Some Notes on the Transfer of Populations,' *Political Quarterly* 14:1 (1943), 363–71.

45 In 1993 the World Bank, prodded by environmentalists in the North, pulled

out of this project, which will displace nearly 170,000 people. The three Indian state governments involved (Gujarat, Maharashtra, and Madhya Pradesh) remain committed, despite a Gujurat High Court stay and the threat of mass suicides in the area. 'Indians Threaten Suicide over Dam,' *Globe and Mail*, 26 April 1994, A12. See in particular William Fisher, ed., *Toward Sustainable Development? Struggling over India's Narmada River* (Armonk, NY: M.E. Sharpe, 1995).

46 Paul Kennedy, *Preparing for the Twenty-First Century* (New York: Random House, 1993), 58.

47 Quoted in Linda Hossie, 'Slipping Environment onto the Agenda,' *Globe and Mail*, 26 May 1993, A10.

48 H.G. Wells, *New Worlds For Old* (London: Archibald Constable, 1908), 267.

Chapter 5. Globalization

1 W. Greider, *One World, Ready or Not: The Manic Logic of Global Capitalism* (New York: Simon and Schuster, 1997). See the book review by M. Miler, 'A Rising Tide Sinks All Boats,' in *The New York Times Book Review*, 19 January 1997, 12.

2 'The Complexities and Contradictions of Globalization,' *Current History* 96:613 (1997), 360–4; 361.

3 See for example, R. Maghroori and B. Ramber, eds., *Globalism versus Realism: International Relations Third Debate* (Boulder, CO: Westview, 1982), where globalism is really a term employed to connote what Keohane and Nye termed 'interdependence.'

4 A. Bergensen, ed., *Studies of the Modern World System* (Toronto: Academic, 1980), 1.

5 *The Study of Global Interdependence: Essays on the Transnationalization of World Affairs* (New York: Nichols, 1980), 1–2.

6 'Globalization: The Great American Non-Debate,' *Current History* 96:613 (1997), 353–9; 353.

7 See Gilbert Winham, 'International Trade Policy in a Globalizing Economy,' *International Journal* 51 (1996), 638–50.

8 Claire Turenne Sjolander, 'The Rhetoric of Globalization: What's in a Wor(l)d?' *International Journal* 51 (1996), 603–16. Note that Sjolander argues that some states have been able to protect themselves from the harsher intrusions of globalization, despite the rhetoric of inevitability produced by Western governments, through neoprotectionist strategies such as voluntary export restraints, orderly marketing arrangements, and the use of anti-

dumping and countervailing duty policies. See her 'Multilateralism, Regionalism, and Unilateralism: International Trade and the Marginalization of the South,' paper presented to the 6th Annual Meeting of the Academic Council on the UN System, Montreal, June 1993; see also J. Bhagwati and H. Patrick, eds., *Aggressive Unilateralism: America's 301 Policy and the World Trading System* (Ann Arbor: University of Michigan Press, 1990).

9 E. Kapstein, 'Workers and the World Economy,' in *Foreign Affairs Agenda: The New Shape of World Politics* (New York: Norton, 1997), 187–205; 189.

10 R. Cox, 'The Global Political Economy and Social Choice,' in D. Drache and M. Gertler, *The New Era of Global Competition: State Policy and Market Power* (Montreal and Kingston: McGill-Queen's University Press, 1991), 335–49; 336.

11 'Fiddling the Figures on World Poverty,' *The Toronto Star*, 1 September 1996, F3.

12 M. Waters, *Globalization* (London: Routledge, 1995), 3.

13 Ibid., 4.

14 R. Volti, *Society and Technological Change*, Second Edition (New York: St. Martin's Press, 1992), 235.

15 Note the popularity of the International Standards Organization (ISO) certification process in industry today.

16 *Turbulence in World Politics* (Princeton: Princeton University Press, 1990), 17.

17 R. Walters and D. Blake, *The Politics of Global Economic Relations*, Fourth Edition (Englewood Cliffs, NJ: Prentice Hall, 1992), 188.

18 See Donald Janelle, 'Central Place Development in a Time-Space Framework,' *Professional Geographer* 20:1 (1969), 5–10; and D. Harvey's seminal *The Condition of Postmodernity: An Enquiry into the Origins of Cultural Change* (Oxford: Blackwell, 1989).

19 See A. Amin and N. Thrift, 'Neo-Marshallian Nodes in Global Networks,' *International Journal of Urban and Regional Research* 16:4 (1992), 571–87.

20 From the Introduction to J. Allen and C. Hamnett, eds., *A Shrinking World? Global Unevenness and Inequality* (New York: Oxford, 1995), 1–9; 8.

21 J.-J. Salomon and A. Lebeau, *Mirages of Development: Science and Technology for the Third Worlds* (Boulder, CO, and London: Lynne Rienner, 1993), 86. See also Paul Kennedy's *Preparing for the Twentieth Century* (New York: Random House, 1993).

22 This according to the UNDP *Human Development Report 1992* (New York: Oxford University Press, 1992), 2.

23 See Vandana Shiva, *Monocultures of the Mind* (London: Zed and Third World Network, 1993).

24 Robert Cox, 'Critical Political Economy,' in Bjorn Hettne, ed., *International*

Political Economy: Understanding Global Disorder (London: Zed, 1995), 41.

25 See J. Brecher, J. Brown Childs, and J. Cutler, *Global Visions: Beyond the New World Order* (Montreal: Black Rose, 1993).

26 See his 'Globalization and Other Stories: The Search for a New Paradigm for International Relations,' *International Journal* 51 (1996), 617.

27 Nef, 50.

28 'Global Perestroika,' in R. Cox with Timothy Sinclair, *Approaches to World Order* (Cambridge: Cambridge University Press, 1996), 301. This follows the Coxian assertion that the state is 'part of a larger and more complex political structure that is the counterpart to international production,' wherein the internationalization of the state followed the replacement of an international exchange economy with one based on production (brought on by capital mobility). See his *Power, Production, and World Order: Social Forces in the Making of History* (New York: Columbia University Press, 1987), 253.

29 *Inside/Outside*, 82.

30 V. Kavolis, 'Contemporary Moral Cultures and "the Return of the Sacred,"' *Sociological Analysis* 49:3 (1988), 203–16; 210–12.

31 R. White, *Global Spin: Probing the Civilization Debate* (Toronto: Dundurn, 1995), 127.

32 Richard Jolly, quoted in J. Stackhouse, 'Canada Is the Best, UN Reports,' *Globe and Mail*, 17 July 1996, A10.

33 R. Reich, *The Work of Nations* (New York: Alfred Knopf, 1991), 8.

34 Canada did this in 1995 when a dispute with Spanish fishing fleets reached the crisis point. See Andrew Cooper, *Canadian Foreign Policy: Old Habits and New Directions* (Scarborough: Prentice Hall/Allyn and Bacon, 1997), 142–72.

35 Stuart Nagel, ed. *Global Policy Studies: International Interaction toward Improving Public Policy* (New York: St. Martin's, 1991), xiii.

36 'A Theoretical Framework for Global Policy Studies,' in ibid.

37 Nef, *op. cit.*, 50.

Selected Readings

Chapter 1. Terminology and Security in World Politics

Arnett, E. *Science and International Security: New Perspectives for a Changing World Order.* Washington: American Association for the Advancement of Science, 1991.

Booth, Ken. *Strategy and Ethnocentrism.* New York: Holmes and Meier, 1979.

– *New Thinking about Strategy and International Security.* London: HarperCollins, 1991.

Brock, L. 'Peace through Parks: The Environment on the Peace Research Agenda.' *Journal of Peace Research* 28:4 (1991), 407–23.

Brown, L. 'Redefining National Security.' Washington: Worldwatch Institute Paper No. 14, Washington, 1977.

Brown, N. 'Ecology and World Security.' *The World Today* 48:3 (1992), 51–4.

Buzan, B. *People, States and Fear: An Agenda for International Security Studies in the Post-Cold War Era.* London: Harvester Wheatsheaf, 1991.

– 'New Patterns of Global Security in the Twenty-First Century.' *International Affairs* 67:3 (1991), 431–51.

Byers, B. 'Ecoregions, State Sovereignty and Conflict?' *Bulletin of Peace Proposals* 22:1 (1991), 65–76.

Campbell, D. *Writing Security: United States Foreign Policy and the Politics of Identity.* Minneapolis: University of Minnesota Press, 1992.

Colinvaux, P. *Fates of Nations: A Biological Theory of History.* New York: Simon and Schuster, 1980.

Crosby, A. *Ecological Imperialism: The Biological Expansion of Europe, 900–1900.* Cambridge: Cambridge University Press, 1986.

Dabelko, G., and D. Dabelko. 'Environmental Security: Issues of Conflict and Redefinitions.' *Environment and Security* 1 (1996), 23–49.

Dalby, S. 'Security, Modernity, Ecology: The Dilemma of a Post-Cold War Security Discourse.' *Alternatives* 17 (1992).

Fawn, R., and J. Larkins. *International Society after the Cold War.* New York: St. Martin's, 1996.

Finnemore, M. *National Interests in International Society.* Ithaca, NY: Cornell University Press, 1996.

Forsythe, B. *International Human Rights.* Lexington: Lexington Books, 1991.

Gonick, L.S., and E. Weisband, eds. *Teaching World Politics: Contending Pedagogies for a New World Order.* Boulder, CO: Westview, 1992.

Gray, C. 'Through a Missile Tube Darkly: "New Thinking" about Nuclear Strategy.' *Political Studies,* 41:4 (1993), 661–71.

Grieco, J. 'Anarchy and the Limits of Cooperation: A Realist Critique of the Newest Liberal Institutionalism.' *International Organization* 42 (1988), 485–507.

Haas, E. 'Words Can Hurt You; Or, Who Said What to Whom about Regimes.' In S. Krasner, *International Regimes* (Ithaca, NY: Cornell University Press, 1983), 23–59.

Halliday, F. 'International Relations: Is There a New Agenda?' *Millennium* 20:1 (1991), 57–72.

Helman, U. 'Environment and the National Interest: An Analytical Survey.' *The Washington Quarterly* 13:4 (1990), 193–206.

Hillal Dessouki, A. 'The Two Spheres of Security.' *The Washington Quarterly* 16:4 (1993), 109–17.

Holst, J. 'Security and the Environment: A Preliminary Exploration.' *Bulletin of Peace Proposals* 20:2 (1989), 123–8.

Kolodziej, E. 'Renaissance in Security Studies? Caveat Lector!' *International Studies Quarterly* 36 (1992), 421–38.

Krause, K., and M. Williams. 'Broadening the Agenda of Security Studies: Politics and Methods.' *Mershon International Studies Review* 40 (1996), 229–54.

Mangold, P. 'Security: New Ideas, Old Ambiguities.' *The World Today* (Royal Institute of International Affairs), 47:2 (1991), 30–3.

Mendlovitz, S., ed. *The Creation of a Just World Order: Preferred Worlds for the 1990s.* New York: Free Press, 1975.

Miller, L. *Global Order: Values and Power in International Politics.* Boulder, CO: Westview, 1985.

Mische, P. 'Ecological Security and the Need to Reconceptualize Sovereignty.' *Alternatives* 14 (1989), 389–429.

Renner, M. *Fighting for Survival: Environmental Decline, Social Conflict, and the New Age of Insecurity.* New York: W.W. Norton and Company, 1996.

Rosenau, J. *Turbulence in World Politics*. Princeton, NY: Princeton University Press, 1990.

Schriver, N. 'International Organization for Environmental Security.' *Bulletin of Peace Proposals* 20:2 (1989), 115–22.

Shaw, T. 'Security Redefined: Unconventional Conflict in Africa.' In S. Wright and J. Brownfoot, eds., *Africa in World Politics: Changing Perspectives* (London: Macmillan, 1987), 17–34.

Shiva, V. *Staying Alive: Women, Ecology and Development*. London: Zed, 1988.

Sjolander, C.T., and W. Cox, eds. *Beyond Positivism: Critical Reflections on International Relations*. Boulder, CO: Lynne Rienner, 1994.

Sorensen, Theodore. 'Rethinking National Security.' *Foreign Affairs* 69:3 (1990), 1–18.

Sprout, H. and M. *Toward a Politics of the Planet Earth*. New York: van Nostrand Reinhold, 1971.

Subrahmanyam, K. 'Alternative Security Doctrines.' *Bulletin of Peace Proposals* 22:1 (1990), 77–85.

Thomas, R. 'Who Is the Enemy? Redefining Security.' *Ecodecision: Environmental Policy Magazine* 9 (1993), 41–4.

Walker, R., and S. Mendlovitz, eds. *Contending Sovereignties: Redefining Political Community*. Boulder, CO: Lynn Reinner, 1990.

Weston, B., ed. *Alternative Security: Living without Nuclear Deterrence*. Boulder, CO: Westview, 1990.

Westing, A. 'The Environmental Component of Comprehensive Security,' *Bulletin of Peace Proposals* 20 (1989), 129–34.

Wolfers, A. 'National Security as an Ambiguous Symbol.' *Political Science Quarterly* 67:4 (1952), 481–502.

Zacher, M. 'Toward a Theory of International Regimes.' *Journal of International Affairs* 44:1 (1990), 139–58.

Chapter 2.   State Violence: Genocide

Andrews, J. *International Protection of Human Rights*. New York: Facts on File, 1987.

Arendt, H. *Eichmann in Jerusalem: A Report of the Banality of Evil*. New York: Viking, 1963.

Bauman, Z. *Modernity and the Holocaust*. Ithaca, NY: Cornell University Press, 1989.

Bernhardt, R., Director. *Encyclopedia of International Law, Volume Eight: Human Rights and the Individual in International Law*. Amsterdam: North-Holland, 1985.

Bond, J.E. *The Rules of Riot: Internal Conflict and the Law of War*. Princeton, NJ: Princeton University Press, 1974.

Brecher, I., ed. *Human Rights, Development and Foreign Policy: Canadian Perspectives*. Halifax: Institute for Research on Public Policy, 1989.

Fairley, H.S. 'State Actors, Humanitarian Intervention and International Law: Reopening the Pandora's Box.' *Georgia Journal of International and Cooperative Law* 10:1 (1980), 29–63.

Falk, R., S. Kim, and S. Mendlovitz, eds. *The United Nations and a Just World Order*. Boulder, CO: Westview, 1991.

Fawcett, E., and H. Newcombe. *United Nations Reform: Looking Ahead after Fifty Years*. Toronto: Science for Peace, 1995.

Fein, H. *Genocide: A Sociological Perspective*. London: Newbury Park, 1993.

Forsythe, D. *The Internationalization of Human Rights*. Lexington: D.C. Heath, 1991.

Fraser, J.M. 'Bosnia and Other Balkan Powder Kegs.' In M.A. Molot and H. von Riekhoff, eds., *Canada among Nations 1994: A Part of the Peace* (Ottawa: Carleton University Press, 1994), 301–22.

Friedman, S., ed. *Holocaust Literature: A Handbook of Critical, Historical, and Literary Writings*. Westport: Greenwood, 1993.

Geldenhuys, D. *Isolated States: A Comparative Analysis*. Cambridge: Cambridge University Press, 1990.

Harff, B. *Genocide and Human Rights: International Legal and Political Issues*. Denver: University of Denver Press, 1984.

Hilberg, R. *The Destruction of the European Jews*. New York: Holmes and Meier, 1983.

Horowitz, I. *Genocide: State Power and Mass Murder*. New Brunswick, New Jersey: Transaction Books, 1976.

Howard, R., and J. Donnelly. 'Human Dignity, Human Rights, and Political Regimes.' *American Political Science Review*. 80:3 (1986), 801–18.

Jackson, R.H. *Quasi-states: Sovereignty, International Relations and the Third World*. Cambridge: Cambridge University Press, 1990.

James, A. *Peacekeeping in International Politics*. New York: St. Martin's Press, 1990.

Job, B., ed. *The Insecurity Dilemma: National Security of Third World States*. Boulder, CO: Lynne Rienner, 1992.

Kansteiner, W. 'From Exception to Exemplum: The New Approach to Nazism and the "Final Solution."' *History and Theory: Studies in the Philosophy of History* 33:2 (1994), 145–71.

Kuper, L. *Genocide*. New Haven: Yale University Press, 1981.

Kushner, T. *The Holocaust and the Liberal Imagination: A Social and Cultural History.* Oxford: Blackwell, 1994.

Lemkin, R. *Axis Rule in Occupied Europe.* Washington: Carnegie Endowment, 1944.

Matas, D. 'Prosecution in Canada for Crimes against Humanity.' *New York Law School Journal of International and Comparative Law* 11 (1991), 347–55.

Matthews, R.O., and C. Pratt. *Human Rights in Canadian Foreign Policy.* Kingston and Montreal: McGill-Queen's University Press, 1988.

McCormick, J., and N. Mitchell. 'Human Rights and Foreign Assistance: An Update.' *Social Science Quarterly* 70 (1989), 969–79.

Melson, R. *Revolution and Genocide: On the Origins of the Armenian Genocide and the Holocaust.* Chicago: University of Chicago Press, 1992.

Moynihan, D.P. *Pandaemonium: Ethnicity in International Politics.* Oxford: Oxford University Press, 1993.

Rawls, J. *A Theory of Justice.* Cambridge: Harvard University Press, 1971.

Roberts, A., and B. Kingsbury, eds. *United Nations, Divided World: The UN's Roles in International Relations.* Oxford: Clarendon Press, 1993.

Robertson, A. *Human Rights in the World: An Introduction to the International Protection of Human Rights.* New York: St. Martin's Press, 1982.

Rowe, P., ed., *The Gulf War 1990–91 in International and English Law.* London: Routledge, 1993.

Schmitz, G., and V. Berry. *Human Rights: Canadian Policy toward Developing Countries.* Ottawa: North-South Institute, 1988.

Shue, H. *Basic Rights: Subsistence, Affluence, and U.S. Foreign Policy.* Princeton, NJ: Princeton University Press, 1980.

Singh, N., and E. McWhinney. *Nuclear Weapons and Contemporary International Law.* Second Edition. Dordrecht: Martinus Nijhoff, 1989.

Steiner, H., and P. Alston. *International Human Rights in Context: Law, Politics, Morals.* Oxford: Oxford University Press, 1996.

Sullivan, M. *Measuring Global Values.* New York: Greenwood, 1991.

Tomasevski, K. *Development Aid and Human Rights.* London: Printer, 1988.

Vincent, R.J. *Nonintervention and International Order.* Princeton, NJ: Princeton University Press, 1974.

Weiss, T., and L. Minear. 'Do International Ethics Matter?: Humanitarian Politics and the Sudan.' *Ethics and International Affairs* 5 (1991), 197–214.

Welch, D. *Justice and the Genesis of War.* Cambridge: Cambridge University Press, 1993.

Wiesel, E. *Dimensions of the Holocaust: Lectures at Northwestern University,* Second Edition. Evanston: Northwestern University Press, 1990.

Chapter 3.   Environmental Degradation: Ecocide

Barnaby, F. 'Environmental Warfare.' *Bulletin of the Atomic Scientists* 32 (1976), 36–43.

Barrett, R., ed. *International Dimensions of the Environmental Crisis.* Boulder, CO: Westview, 1982.

Bennett, O., ed., *Greenwar: Environment and Conflict.* London: Panos Institute, 1991.

Butts, K. 'National Security, the Environment and DOD.' *Environmental Change and Security Project,* Woodrow Wilson Center, Issue 2 (1996), 22–7.

Clark, C. 'The Economics of Overexploitation.' *Science* 181 (1973), 630–4.

Commission on Global Governance. *Our Global Neighbourhood: The Report of the Commission on Global Governance.* Oxford: University of Oxford Press, 1995.

Devall, B., and G. Sessions. *Deep Ecology: Living As If Nature Mattered.* Salt Lake City: Peregrine Smith, 1985.

Cranna, M., ed. *The True Cost of Conflict.* London: Earthscan, 1994.

Dalby, S. 'The Environment as Geopolitical Threat: Reading Robert Kaplan's "Coming Anarchy."' *Ecumene* 3:4 (1996), 472–96.

Davis, M. 'The Dead West: Ecocide in Marlboro Country.' *New Left Review* 200 (July/August, 1993), 49–74.

DeBardeleben, J., and J. Hannigan, eds. *Environmental Security and Quality after Communism: Eastern Europe and the Soviet Successor States.* Boulder, CO: Westview, 1995.

Deibert, R. 'From Deep Black to Green? Demystifying the Military Monitoring of the Environment.' *Environmental Change and Security Project,* Woodrow Wilson Center, Issue 2 (1996), 28–32.

Dycus, S. *National Defense and the Environment.* University Press of New England, 1996.

Faber, D. *Environment under Fire: Imperialism and the Ecological Crisis in Central America.* New York: Monthly Review, 1993.

Fadiman, C., and J. White, ed. *Ecocide ... And Thoughts toward Survival.* New York: James Feel and Associates, in collaboration with the Center for the Study of Democratic Institutions, 1971.

Falk, R. 'Environmental Warfare and Ecocide.' *Bulletin of Peace Proposals* 4 (1973), 1–17.

Feshbach, M., and A. Friendly. *Ecocide in the USSR: Health and Nature under Siege.* New York: Basic Books, 1992.

Galtung, J. *Environment, Development, and Military Activity: Towards Alternative Security Doctrines.* Oslo: Universitetsforlaget, 1982.

Goldblat, J. 'The Environmental Warfare Convention: How Meaningful Is It?' *Ambio* 6 (1977), 216–21.

Haig, B. 'Why We Must Accept Nuclear Winter Theory.' *Bulletin of Peace Proposals* 20:1 (1989), 81–8.

Homer-Dixon, T. 'On the Threshold: Environmental Changes and Causes of Acute Conflict.' *International Security* 16:2 (1991), 76–116.

Juda, L. 'Negotiating a Treaty on Environmental Modification Warfare: The Convention on Environmental Warfare and Its Impact upon Arms Control Negotiations.' *International Organization* 32:4 (1978), 975–92.

Kelly, K. 'Declaring War on the Environment: The Failure of International Environmental Treaties during the Persian Gulf War.' *The American University Journal of International Law and Policy* 7:4 (1992), 921–50.

Lewallen, J. *Ecology of Destruction: Indochina.* Baltimore: Penguin, 1971.

Litfin, K. 'Sovereignty in World Ecopolitics.' *Mershon International Studies Review* 41 (1997), 167–204.

McMahon, K. 'Arctic Ecocide.' *Peace Magazine* (Toronto), 5:3 (June 1989), 16–17.

Mies, M., and V. Shiva. *Ecofeminism.* Halifax: Fernwood Publications, 1993.

Neilands, J., et al. *Harvest of Death: Chemical Warfare in Vietnam and Cambodia.* New York: Free Press, 1972.

Peterson, J., ed. *The Aftermath: The Human and Ecological Consequences of Nuclear War.* New York: Pantheon, 1983.

Roach, J.A. 'The Laws of War and the Protection of the Environment.' *Environment and Security* 2 (1997).

Robinson, J.P. 'The Effects of Weapons on Ecosystems.' *United Nations Environment Programme Studies, Volume One.* Toronto: Permagon, 1979.

Rowe, P., ed. *The Gulf War 1990–91 in International and English Law.* London: Routledge and Sweet & Maxwell, 1993.

Rueter, T., and T. Kalil. 'Nuclear Strategy and Nuclear Winter.' *World Politics* 43 (July 1991), 587–607; 590.

Sagan, C. 'Nuclear War and Climatic Catastrophe: Some Policy Implications.' *Foreign Affairs* 62 (Winter 1982/4), 257–92.

Schell, J. *The Fate of the Earth.* New York: Knopf, 1982.

– *The Military Half: An Account of Destruction in Quang Ngai and Quang Tin.* New York: Knopf, 1968.

Schiefer, B., ed. *Verifying Obligations Respecting Arms Control and the Environment: A Post Gulf War Assessment.* Saskatoon: University of Saskatchewan, 1992.

Shulman, S. *The Threat at Home: Confronting the Toxic Legacy of the U.S. Military.* Boston: Beacon, 1992.

Schrijver, N. 'Nuclear Weapons Tests, Arms Control, and the Environment: The 1995 World Court Case and Beyond.' *Environment and Security* 2 (1997).

Stevens, R. *The Trail: A History of the Ho Chi Minh Trail and the Role of Nature in the War in Viet Nam.* New York: Garland, 1993.

Theorin, B. 'Military Resources to the Environment.' *Bulletin of Peace Proposals* 23:2 (1992), 119–22.

Turco, R.P., et al. 'Nuclear Winter: Global Consequences of Multiple Nuclear Explosions.' *Science* 23 (December 1983), 1283–92.

Weisberg, B., ed. *Ecocide in Indochina: The Ecology of War.* San Francisco: Canfield Press, 1970.

Westing, A. 'Environmental Warfare.' *Environmental Law: Northwestern School of Lewis and Clark College* 15:4 (1985), 645–66.

– ed. *Global Resources and International Conflict: Environmental Factors in Strategic Policy and Action.* Oxford: Oxford University Press, 1986.

– ed. *Cultural Norms, War and the Environment.* Oxford: Oxford University Press, 1988.

Williams, J. 'Land Mines: Dealing with the Environmental Impact.' *Environment and Security* 2 (1997).

Chapter 4.   Population Displacement: Refugees

Abell, N.A. 'The Impact of International Migration on Security and Stability.' *Canadian Foreign Policy* 4:1 (1996), 83–110.

Appleyard, Reginald. *International Migration: Challenge for the Nineties.* Geneva: IOM, 1991.

Blight, J. and T. Weiss. 'Must the Grass Still Suffer? Some Thoughts on Third World Conflicts after the Cold War.' *Third World Quarterly* 13:2 (1992), 229–53.

Buehrig, E. *The UN and the Palestinian Refugees: A Study in Nonterritorial Administration.* Bloomington: Indiana University Press, 1971.

Charlesworth, H., C. Chinkin, and S. Wright. 'Feminist Approaches to International Law.' *The American Journal of International Law* 85 (October–November, 1991), 613–45.

Cohen, R. *Human Rights Protection for Internally Displaced Persons.* Washington: RPG, 1991.

Daes, E.I., ed. *Status of the Individual and Contemporary International Law: Promotion, Protection and Restoration of Human Rights at National, Regional and International Levels.* New York: United Nations, 1992.

Davies, J. *Displaced Peoples and Refugee Studies: A Resource Guide.* Refugee Studies Programme, Oxford University. London: Hans Zell, 1990.

Deng, Francis. *Protecting the Dispossessed: A Challenge for the International Community.* Washington, DC: Brookings Institution, 1993.

Dirks, G. 'International Migration in the Nineties: Causes and Consequences.' *International Journal* 48:2 (1993), 191–214.

FAO. *Sustainable Development and the Environment: FAO Policies and Actions, Stockholm 1972 – Rio 1992.* Rome, 1993.

Glassman, J. 'Counter-Insurgency, Ecocide and the Production of Refugees: Warfare as a Tool of Modernization.' *Refuge* 12:1 (1992), 27–30.

Gurtov, M. 'Open Borders: A Global Humanist Approach to the Refugee Crisis.' *World Development* 19:5 (1991), 485–96.

Hansen, A. 'Refugee Dynamics: Angolans in Zambia, 1966 to 1972.' *International Migration Review* 15:3 (1981), 175–94.

Hastedt, G., and K. Knickrehm. 'Predicting State Response to Refugees: The Decision Logic of Receiving States.' In same, eds., *Toward the Twenty-First Century: A Reader in World Politics* (Englewood Cliffs, NJ: Prentice Hall, 1994), 382–9.

Hengeveld, H. *Understanding Atmospheric Change.* Ottawa: Environment Canada, State of the Environment Report 91, 1991.

Hubbel, D. and N. Rajesh, 'Not Seeing the People for the Forest: Thailand's Program of Reforestation by Forced Eviction.' *Refuge* 12:1 (1992), 20–1.

Huysmans, J. 'Migrants as a Security Problem: Dangers of "Securitizing" Societal Issues.' In R. Miles and D. Thranhardt, eds., *Migration and European Integration: The Dynamics of Inclusion and Exclusion.* London: Pinter, 1995.

Independent Commission on International Humanitarian Issues (ICIHI). *Refugees: The Dynamics of Displacement.* London: Zed Books, 1986.

Jacobson, J. *Environmental Refugees: A Yardstick of Habitability.* Washington, DC: Worldwatch Institute, 1988.

Kane, H. 'The Hour of Departure: Forces That Create Refugees and Migrants.' *Worldwatch Paper No. 125,* Washington, DC: Worldwatch Institute, 1995.

Kavanagh, B., and K. Lonergan. *Environmental Degradation, Population Displacement and Global Security: An Overview of the Issues.* Ottawa: Royal Society of Canada, 1992.

Keen, D. *Refugees: Rationing the Right to Life.* Oxford: Oxford University Press, 1992.

Kennedy, P. *Preparing for the Twenty-First Century.* New York: Random House, 1993.

Magotte, J. *Disposable People? The Plight of Refugees.* New York: Orbis, 1992.

Martin, S. *Refugee Women.* London: Zed Books, 1992.

Melander, G., and P. Nobel, eds. *International Legal Instruments on Refugees in Africa.* Uppsala: SIAS, 1979.

Newland, Kathryn. *Refugees: The New International Politics of Displacement.* Washington, DC: Worldwatch Institute, 1981.

North-South Institute. 'Refugees: Humanitarian Assistance in Harsh Times.' N-S Institute briefing, November 1982, Ottawa.

Ogata, Sadako. 'The UN Response to the Growing Refugee Crisis.' *Japan Review of International Affairs* 7:3 (1993), 202–15.

Potter, E. 'The Challenge of Responding to International Migration.' *Canadian Foreign Policy* 4:1 (1996), 1–22.

Richmond, A. 'Open and Closed Borders: Is the New World Order Creating a System of Global Apartheid?' *Refuge* 13:1 (1993), 6–10.

Ristelhueber, R. *Au secours des refugies: l'ouevre de l'Organisation internationale pour les refugies.* Paris: Presences, 1951.

Rogers, R. 'The Future of Refugee Flows and Policies.' *International Migration Review* 36:4 (1992), 1112–143.

Rudwin, L., ed. *Shelter, Settlement and Development.* Boston: Allen and Unwin, 1987.

Stoett, P.J. 'International Mechanisms for Addressing International Migration.' *Canadian Foreign Policy* 4:1 (1996), 111–38.

UNEP and UNCHS. *Environmental Guidelines for Settlements Planning and Management.* 3 volumes. Geneva: Author, 1987.

UNHCR. *Images of Exile.* Geneva: Author, 1991.

– *A Mandate to Protect and Assist Refugees.* Geneva: Author, 1971.

Weiner, M. 'Security, Stability and International Migration.' *International Security* (Winter 1992–93), 91–126.

Zolberg, J. 'Un reflet du monde: les migrations internationales en perspective historique.' *Revu Études Internationales* 24:1 (1993), 17–29.

Chapter 5.   Globalization

Addo, H., et al., *Development and Social Transformation: Reflections on the Global Problematique.* Boulder, CO: Lynne Reinner, 1985.

Adriaansen, W., and J. Waardensburg, eds. *A Dual World Economy.* Groningen: Wolters-Noordhoff, 1989.

Afshar, H. *Women, Development and Survival in the Third World.* New York: Feminist Press, 1991.

Baldwin, D. 'Security Studies and the End of the Cold War.' *World Politics* 48 (1995), 117–41.

Barber, B. 'Jihad vs. McWorld.' *Atlantic* 269 (March, 1992), 53–63.

Bienfeld, M. 'The New World Order: Echoes of a New Imperialism.' *Third World Quarterly* 15:1 (1994).

Cameron, D., and F. Houle, eds. *Canada and the New International Division of Labour.* Ottawa: University of Ottawa Press, 1985.

Carnoy, M., et al., eds. *The Global Economy in the Information Age.* University Park: Pennsylvania State University Press, 1993.

Chase-Dunn, C. *Global Formation: The Structures of the World Economy.* Cambridge: Basil Blackwell, 1991.

Conklin D., and T. Courchene, eds. *Canadian Trade at a Crossroads: Options for New International Agreements.*Toronto: Economic Council of Ontario, 1985.

Czempiel, E-O., and J. Rosenau, eds.*Global Changes and Theoretical Challenges: Approaches to World Politics for the 1990s.* Lexington: Lexington Books, 1989.

Del Rosso, S. 'The Insecure State: Reflections on *the State* and *Security* in a Changing World.' *Daedalus* 124:2 (1995), 175–207.

Drache, D., and M. Gertler, eds. *The New Era of Global Competition: State Policy and Market Power.* Montreal and Kingston: McGill-Queen's University Press, 1991.

Drury, S. 'The End of History and the New World Order.' *International Journal* 48:1 (1993), 80–99.

Galtung, J. *The True Worlds: A Transnational Perspective.* New York: Free Press, 1980.

Gill, S., ed. *Gramsci, Historical Materialism, and International Relations.* Cambridge: Cambridge University Press, 1993.

Gordon, D.M. 'The Global Economy: New Edifice or Crumbling Foundation?' *New Left Review* 168 (1988), 24–64.

Griffin Cohen, M. *Free Trade and the Future of Women's Work: Manufacturing and Service Industries.* Toronto: Garamond, 1987.

Haggard, S., and R. Kaufman, eds. *The Politics of Economic Adjustment: International Constraints, Distributive Conflicts, and the State.* Princeton, NJ: Princeton University Press, 1992.

Head, I. *On the Hinge of History: The Mutual Vulnerability of South and North.* Toronto: University of Toronto Press, 1991.

Holm, H.H., and G. Sorensen, eds. *Whose World Order? Uneven Globalization and the End of the Cold War.* Boulder, CO: Westview Press, 1995.

Hufner, K. and J. Naumann. 'Are the Moral and Value Foundations of Multilateralism Changing?' *International Political Science Review* 11:3 (1990), 323–34.

Kardam, N. *Bringing Women In: Women's Issues in International Development Programs.* Boulder, CO: Lynne Rienner, 1990.

Karliner, J. *The Corporate Planet: Ecology and Politics in the Age of Globalization.* San Francisco: Sierra Club, 1997.

Katzenstein, P., ed. *Between Power and Plenty: Foreign Economic Policies of Advanced Industrial States.* Madison: University of Wisconsin Press, 1978.

King, A.D., ed. *Culture, Globalization and the World System*. London: Macmillan, 1991.

Kratochwil, F. *Rules, Norms, and Decisions: On the Conditions of Practical and Legal Reasoning in International Relations and Domestic Affairs*. New York: Cambridge University Press, 1989.

Lele, J., and W. Tettey, eds. *Asia: Who Pays for Growth? Women, Environment and Popular Movements*. Aldershot: Dartmouth, 1996.

Lieber, R. 'Oil and Power after the Gulf War.' *International Security* 17:1 (1992), 155–76.

Lopez, G., et al. 'The Global Tide.' *Bulletin of the Atomic Scientists* (July/August 1995), 33–9.

Mansbach, R. 'The World Turned Upside Down.' *The Journal of East Asian Affairs* 7:2 (1993), 451–97.

Massiah, J., ed. *Women in Developing Economies: Making Visible the Invisible*. New York: Berg, 1992.

Mowlana, H. *Global Information and World Communication: New Frontiers in International Relations*. New York: Longman, 1986.

Naisbitt, J. *Global Paradox: The Bigger the World Economy, the More Powerful Its Smallest Players*. New York: Avon, 1994.

O'Brien, R. *Global Financial Integration: The End of Geography*. London: Pinter, 1991.

Ohmae, K. *The Borderless World: Power and Strategy in the Interlinked Economy*. London: Fontana, 1990.

Pitroda, S. 'From GATT to WTO: The Institutionalization of World Trade.' *Harvard International Review*, Spring 1995, 46–7.

Redclift, M. *Sustainable Development: Exploring the Contradictions*. London: Methuen, 1987.

Ritzer, G. *The McDonaldization of Society*. Thousand Oaks: Pine Forge, 1993.

Robinson, W. 'Globalization, the World System, and "Democracy Promotion" in U.S. Foreign Policy.' *Theory and Society* 25 (1996).

Roche, D. *A Bargain for Humanity: Global Security by 2000*. Edmonton: University of Alberta Press, 1993.

Rosenau, J. *Turbulence in World Politics*. Princeton, NJ: Princeton University Press, 1990.

Saskia, S. *Losing Control? Sovereignty in an Age of Globalization*. New York: Columbia University Press, 1996.

Sassens, S. *The Global City: New York, London, Tokyo*. Princeton, NJ: Princeton University Press, 1991.

Shaw, T. 'The New World Disorder.' *Third World Quarterly* 15:1 (1994).

Sheperd, O.W., and V.P. Nanda, eds. *Human Rights and Third World Development*. Westport: Greenwood, 1985.

Stubbs, R, and G. Underhill, eds. *Political Economy and the Changing Global Order*. Toronto: McClelland & Stewart, 1994.

United States, Department of State. *Country Reports on Human Rights Practices*. Washington, DC: various years.

van den Berghe, P., ed. *State Violence and Ethnicity*. Niwot, CO: University Press of Colorado, 1990.

Weiss, T., and L. Minear. 'Do International Ethics Matter? Humanitarian Politics and the Sudan.' *Ethics and International Affairs* 5 (1991), 197–214.

Index